Prais

COMMERCIAL TRUCK SUCCESS

"I finished a quick read of your publication and truly enjoyed and admired it very much. You have focused on all of the important details for a truck dealer to become successful.

I would like to purchase a hard copy as soon as it becomes available. As you can imagine, I would like to utilize excerpts, ideas and quotes from your publication in some of my future training classes.

I like what I see and this publication will be a great asset for our industry. I'm anxious to implement several of the areas in future seminars. Great job."

Taylor Steinberg, Corporate Sales Trainer, Knapheide Manufacturing

"It's about time someone unlocked the "secrets" to harvesting the rewards of the Commercial Marketplace. All it takes is a plan, a little diligence and some brains. Well, you have taken care of part three for any interested parties; your work can only improve the way resources are expended and sales are consummated.

Once again, my hat is off to you for this accomplishment. It was kind of you to send me an advance copy soliciting my feedback; all that I have to say is: "Yours is a job well done." On behalf of myself—but also undoubtedly for those of us toiling in this marketplace—a very sincere thank you!"

Dudley De Zonia, President, Royal Truck Bodies

"Terry Minion has taught me virtually everything I know about running a commercial truck department. As one of the top volume commercial departments in the Northern California Region, I can honestly say Terry knows what he's talking about.

This is a 'Must Read' for any dealer, whether you're a complete novice, or a well-seasoned dealer with a viable existing commercial operation. You will benefit greatly from this no nonsense approach to understanding and running a commercial truck department.

As dealers, we may play it safe with the 'vanilla milkshake' approach to inventory. But as Terry points out, there are many other options to set you apart from your competition and at the same time eliminate the 'fear factor'. And he should know. He's been there and done that in multiple situations.

Terry takes you through a practical approach to learning what makes a dealership successful. Discover the many other opportunities within the finance, parts and service departments, maintenance, and management. If you are not sure how to implement this cohesiveness... this book is for you!

Whether you want to add $100,000 or $1,000,000 to your bottom line, you will benefit greatly from this 'how to' on commercial trucks."

Greg Martin, Commercial Truck Manager,
Platinum Chevrolet

"Terry exposes all the elements needed to run a 'successful' Commercial Truck operation with his many years of experience and the expertise gained from the trials and tribulations of working in the trenches and studying the practices that create the best environment of success in this Industry—all that is needed is a willing participant......"

Mike Soich, Knapheide Manufacturing

"After reading your book, I am wondering if you live in my attic. Wow. For the past 15 years I have been trying to put into words how to sell commercial and fleet accounts. You have nailed it. I was trying to find something wrong with your book. I came up blank."

Bill Shulack, Commercial/Fleet Manager, Harold Zeigler Automotive Group

"I have known, worked with, and worked for Terry Minion for approximately 22 years. When I first started my career in Commercial Vehicle Sales Terry was my employer and my mentor. He remains my mentor to this day. He has a complete knowledge of all aspects of how to successfully start and run a dealership commercial sales division within a dealership. The readers of this book are fortunate to have him share his experience, talents and abilities through this work. If you follow his guidelines it will save you countless thousands of dollars as well as much mental and emotional grief. With Terry's help, training and guidance I was able to achieve great success for both myself and my employing dealerships. If you are contemplating entering the niche market of commercial vehicle sales you must have this book as a complete reference guide on how to succeed and avoid the pit falls that you will only learn from the School Of Hard Knock's."

Ron Reinhold, Commercial Truck/Fleet Manager, Team Chevrolet

"I've been involved in the commercial vehicle business for more than 25 years. During this period I have had the pleasure of knowing and working with Terry Minion in a number of different capacities for close to 20 years. I can unequivocally say Terry

is recognized as an accomplished professional by his peers and colleagues.

His book would be a great resource for anyone in the industry. It provides the reader with a realistic perspective of how to develop and maintain a commercial vehicle department within the framework of an automotive dealership environment."

Harry E Larkin, Commercial Financial Services Mgr, Western Region at Nissan Motor Acceptance Corporation

"Commercial Truck Success is a treasure chest of information on how to build a successful Commercial Department for any dealership. The unique B2B components of selling work trucks are highlighted throughout."

Kathryn Schifferle, MBA, Executive Director, National Ford Truck Club.

"Terry Minion approached me when I had just started a commercial truck sales team at my dealership. After listening to Terry about how he had personally done what I was attempting to do, I thought I can do this with Terry's help. We forecasted how we would build our sales team and our sales over the next three years. Everything we set goals for happened with Terry's guidance."

Paul Brown, *Commercial/Fleet Manager, Larry Geweke Ford*

Commercial
Truck Success

Building or Rebuilding an Effective, Successful, and Profitable
Commercial Truck Operation within a Retail Auto Dealership

2nd Edition

Terry R. Minion

DocUmeant *Publishing*
244 5th Avenue
Suite G-200
NY, NY 10001
646-233-4366
www.DocUmeantPublishing.com

Published by
DocUmeant Publishing
244 5th Avenue, Suite G-200
NY, NY 10001

Phone: 646-233-4366

Wendy VanHatten, VanHatten Writing Services
Copy Editor

www. WendyVanhatten.com

Ginger Marks, DocUmeant Designs
Design & Layout

www.DocUmeantDesigns.com

ISBN13: 978-1-937801-63-2
ISBN10: 1937801632

DEDICATION

I dedicate this book to all those hearty souls who do the work that requires the need for commercial trucks. It is these people that I have focused on serving first. The dealers I have worked for only allowed that to take place to the best of my ability and skill.

Terry Minion

CONTENTS

FOREWORD

As I was approached to write this foreword I was somewhat at a loss what to write. The first thing I did was to call the editor of this book and ask, "What is expected in a foreword?" She explained to me it was basically a short document that validates the author.

Terry Minion has plenty to say about commercial trucks and building successful businesses around them. His expertise goes further than commercial trucks. I can attest to that. However, commercial truck success is what this book showcases. After thinking about it, I figured the best way to validate our author is to tell you the story of how I first met him, and how over time he has validated himself to me.

I first met Terry in 1999 when he made a brief stop at a dealership where I was working in Northern California. He briefly introduced himself as a representative for a commercial body manufacturer out of southern California, left me a card, and was on his way. To tell you the truth, I vaguely remember the meeting at all.

As a new quickly-growing salesman in my twenties I was successfully figuring out how to sell cars and trucks. I was studying the likes of Joe Verde and realized clients that I sold business vehicles to were more loyal and less of a hassle once you earned their business.

When I needed a quote on a truck body, I tried calling Terry, my body rep for northern California. Leaving him a message, I expected a prompt return call. That didn't happen—at least not in the time frame I expected. Since I needed to sell these trucks I began to call the body manufacturer directly. With great customer service from the internal sales lady, she became my go to person for quotes and body orders.

I made sure I gave her an ear full about the rep here in northern California, too! She assured me very politely that he was probably busy and didn't intend to offend me. Later I found out I was "small potatoes," because I didn't keep any commercial inventory in stock and only ordered when I was sure a unit was sold.

A few years went by and I plugged along successfully selling vehicles (many commercial). Then, for a second time I was introduced to Terry. He had started a consulting program for commercial truck departments and our dealership was going to be one of the dealers. Now was my chance to give him an earful about my feelings for him and his lousy customer service. He laughed. I continued to tell him how much better some of the representatives were at the main office in southern California, which made him laugh even more. I was irritated to say the least until he went on to explain to me that he used to be the director of sales and marketing for the entire company and had hired and trained everyone I was raving about.

This is where I slowly began to pull my foot out of my mouth.

We developed a relationship working together building a successful commercial truck operation at my dealership. He became my friend and mentor for commercial truck sales. At this point, I thought he was a very good and proactive body manufacturer representative. He wasn't trying to get me to buy more bodies; he was trying to teach me how to create a successful department, which is exactly what this book is about.

After I left that dealership, I still stayed in touch with Terry. I tried a stint at real estate (2007, wasn't a good year to jump into that market!) and Terry saw me struggling. He connected me with a job running a commercial truck operation at another dealership where he was consulting in the bay area. He continued his mentoring with me to help develop the department teaching me inventory management, prospecting, and dealership integration. Guess what? It all worked.

I was becoming a commercial truck guru under the apprenticeship of Terry Minion.

Due to upper management changes, my success was short lived at that dealership and I was looking for a new venue. That's when Terry asked if I would like to join his little company he had just started, and I agreed.

On our first day as business partners we sat in Terry's home office and told our life stories to each other to gain a better perspective. This is when I found out that Terry had personally not only created one but two of the most successful commercial truck departments on the west coast. He started in the automobile business in 1972, managing since 1975. (Both well before I was even born ...)

Over the past few years in this Commercial Truck Success venture I have learned that Terry has been on the front lines as well as managing retail and commercial operations. Interestingly enough, many of the successful people in this region were either hired into the business by Terry, mentored by Terry, or at least know of him. He is a legend in his own right, and even though I find myself mostly in his shadow, there is no place I'd rather be.

I trust you will benefit from this book about Terry's duplicatable success, and hope this validates Terry—salesperson, manager, mentor, teacher, business partner, and friend; he has been all to me.

Ryan Stone
Partner, Upward Trend Management Services

WELCOME

Thank you for buying this book. My name is Terry Minion and I am writing this book from my perspective of years of learning and growing in the commercial truck market.

Operating a successful and profitable Commercial Truck Department within the retail auto dealership arena is the focus of this book. I have started two Commercial Truck Departments and made them number one in their market area—even a very wide regional market area. Having gathered and perfected that knowledge, I have taught other dealers to do the same thing.

The main reason for this book is that in my experience and travels I have seen the vast majority of Commercial Truck Departments within dealerships fail to be the profit centers they could be. In fact in many dealerships, the department has become an anchor, actually draining profits and resources from the overall operation. As a result of my success in and study of this market, I have developed strategies and systems that can assist any dealer to become much more successful in this unique, interesting, and profitable market.

Who Is The Target Audience For this Book?

This book is slanted toward the auto dealership dealer since this is the person that is generally the decision maker within that organization and also typically the leader, whether in spirit or in truth. In addition, others within the dealership organization may find this material very helpful, such as general managers, sales managers, and commercial/fleet managers. Many times the dealer is influenced by the other managers to entertain a change in business thinking, so this will be helpful toward that end where commercial trucks are concerned.

Other people associated with dealers, whether body companies or other such vendors could also benefit. There are a number of ideas and strategies that I think would benefit a wider audience.

Throughout the book, most of the time, I am speaking to the dealer or executive managers, and sometimes it may seem that I'm talking to the commercial/fleet manager, as in the chapter about the Business Office. I think the reasons will become obvious as you read.

In any case, the purpose of the book is to instill the idea that a Commercial Truck Department can be a huge benefit to a dealership and its growth. This book demonstrates the benefits as well as a plan to have the dealership be successful from the beginning, or recreate it with a better plan than before.

Why Listen To Me?

A very brief history of my experience: Prior to entering the auto business, I worked at a landscape supply company driving commercial trucks and operating equipment, then became a journeyman auto mechanic in the Air Force. After my tour in the service, and not wanting to continue as a mechanic, I began a new career as a totally 'green' sales person in the automobile business. I started at a Chevy dealership in 1972 at age 22, became sales manager in January 1975 and except for leaving the auto business for three years (1980-82), was a sales manager, commercial truck manager, general sales manager until 1997. At that point, I went to work for a major truck body manufacturer for 10 years and in January 2008 began my own consulting and marketing businesses, Commercial Truck Success and Upward Trend Management Services, LLC.

After I started the first Commercial Truck Department in June 1989, our dealership became number one in our market region. In January 1993, I began the second operation. With the accumulated experience and knowledge, I was able to take this operation from non-existent to the number two commercial Chevy dealer in just over a year in the Pacific Coast Region, which is from Alaska to Bakersfield, California including Northern Nevada and Hawaii. The second year, we went to number one and consistently remained in the top 50 dealers nationwide. That was done in a city with 80,000 people. People that I hired and taught went on to begin their own commercial truck operations at other dealerships with similar or even greater results.

During my tenure with the truck body manufacturer, I used my expertise in the commercial market to help dealers who stocked upfitted commercial trucks. In 2005, I began a much more focused long-term consulting program with five selected dealers, as I helped them grow faster and more effectively. I was testing my methods with a new group of dealers, testing some new materials as well, and helping the company I worked for at the same time. I gained a great deal of experience consulting with dealers in the three years that followed, prior to starting my own business.

I have developed websites about commercial trucks offering free valuable information, including a book on sales I wrote in 1990. Also, I have developed a popular blog and bi-monthly newsletter which goes out to almost every state in the U.S. Our Commercial Truck Success Blog is our most popular and varied product that, as of this writing, gets over 100,000 hits per month and 13,000 page views per month.

All along my travels, I am committed to sharing things I've learned and helping anyone interested in learning more about commercial trucks, whether a dealer, manager, sales person, or end user.

In addition, our company builds websites, blogs, manages social media, creates videos, and much more for commercial truck dealerships, retail dealerships, body companies, truck accessory companies, and many other kinds of businesses.

My experience is from many different perspectives having been in different positions in and around the auto dealership venue. It is not past experience, but continuing experience, for I am still very involved with commercial trucks, dealerships, and other related businesses.

For several years I have written a daily inspirations blog and email.

That means I know what I write about. But, I also add that there are a lot of ways to get something done, and I am sharing what I've learned in hopes that it may benefit you.

How Will This Book Help?

This book is designed to offer a detailed overview and strategy for improving any commercial truck operation. Especially, it will help those dealers who are thinking about getting into this market or who have been dabbling in it. Dealers will understand how a commercial truck operation can be dramatically improved and how they can grow it as quickly as possible, with profit.

First, I offer an overview of the commercial truck market and how it fits or does not fit within the dealership structure. I go into some detail in this. Even if you're not an avid reader and you only read this section, you will gain much value from this overview.

Next, I take you through each of the various aspects of a good commercial truck operation explaining the values of that department and the values to the dealership as a whole. I talk about inventory, personnel, service and parts, the business office, training, marketing and integration, and more. I discuss aggressive strategies for those looking to build significant operations as well as conservative, yet profitable, ideas for those less adventurous.

This book is meant to assist the dealers who are unsure, those who have started but are disappointed in results, and those who are thinking about getting into this market. It is meant to encourage and instruct and to offer systems and methods that make sense within a retail dealership operation. As the reader you will understand how that is different and how to use that difference to your best advantage.

Finally, I wrap it up with a summary, some links and suggested contacts, along with an opportunity to get to know our company's services better.

If only one dealership who bought this book used it to create—or recreate—an efficient, successful, and profitable commercial truck operation within their dealership, it will have been worth every effort to create.

It is my joy to serve you!

ACKNOWLEDGEMENTS

When I think about my involvement with commercial trucks, I can think of so many to thank including my mom and grandparents for getting me some sweet Tonka trucks to start me on the right track.

Later, when I had an opportunity to drive them, I have to thank Don Camp who let me get to know dump trucks and skip loaders and all that fun.

Then after entering the career world, I relished the opportunity offered by Karl Esposti and Barry Biddulph to recreate their defunct Commercial Accounts Department beginning in 1989. This led to another time where Doug and Dwight Woodard let me 'play' with trucks at their dealership and perfect my new found joy.

Later still, I thank Ken Lindt for allowing and encouraging me to become a truck body guy. I enjoyed ten years of fun calling on dealers and working with them to have even more fun in commercial trucks.

I cannot forget to thank the producers and associates such as *Chevrolet, GMC, Ford, Isuzu Truck,* and *RAM* who have all helped play a part.

Today, I am still thanking all of them in my new found joy of my own business and knowing that each played an important part in this. I have truly enjoyed being a part of commercial trucks and all the wonderful people I've had the pleasure to come to know and work with.

Thank you also to my partner, Ryan Stone for continually encouraging me with his enthusiastic participation in our endeavors.

I want to also thank Wendy VanHatten for her encouragement and expertise in editing, direction, nurturing, and advising toward completion of this project that was on the table for so many years.

CHAPTER ONE

OVERVIEW

A Bit of History

The commercial vehicle market has always been with us. People have always had the need to transport cargo or carry tools to a remote jobsite since the beginning of transportation. Through the 1800s, the commercial truck market consisted of wagons pulled by animals, then the railroad was introduced. I remember reading somewhere that until the train came in the 1830s it was a three mile per hour world.

Knapheide Manufacturing, the largest truck body manufacturer in the United States, began their company in 1848 as a wagon manufacturer. They carried that into the 20th century before leaving wagons behind for the newer inventions of the automobile and truck.

Since the early 1900s, trucks have been an active part of commerce throughout the world. It is trucks that have helped change the American and world lifestyle so dramatically by offering low cost, efficient methods of transporting goods, and providing services.

When I got into the auto business in 1972, having been an auto mechanic prior to that, trucks were around, but not nearly as plentiful or popular as they are today. I remember my manager having a year-long contest to see how many of us could sell just two trucks per month for the year. Just two. Few made it. Cars were much more popular and trucks were ... just things you needed for work.

Then in the mid-1970s, trucks began changing and became more car-like by including many comfort and convenience options, more attractive designs, interior trim upgrades, and so on. Within just a few years the pickup truck began to show up as an auto manufacturer's highest selling line as well the most profitable. They became so popular and so nicely equipped that many forms of trucks came from this change in pickups, such as the Sport Utility Vehicle (SUV), crossovers, luxury vans, and luxury midsize and compact pickups.

In the late 1980s and early 1990s manufacturers began putting more focus on the light-duty commercial truck market. It really got going with *Chevrolet's* CSV (Commercial Specialty Vehicle) program in 1994 to create and expand commercial truck focused operations within dealerships across the country. This has changed into their Business Central theme as of this writing. *Ford* developed a similar strategy with what is now their Business Preferred Network program and *RAM* with their BUSINESS*LINK* program for dealers.

This led to expansion of the bailment pool system where truck manufacturers stocked empty chassis at various key body manufacturer and upfitter's locations. This was to expedite the sale of upfitted commercial trucks and satisfy the increasing demand for popular work trucks. The bailment pool system existed long before these changes, but it was minute in comparison with what it is today.

Today this bailment pool system is helping dealers and end users get product more quickly and efficiently. Some vehicle manufacturers have continually expanded their commercial truck product offerings in this growing market segment.

The modern commercial truck market where auto dealerships are concerned is relatively new and began in the early 1990s. This change in stocking upfitted commercial trucks at retail dealerships has grown so much. In the 1970s you would be hard pressed to find a dealer who stocked upfitted commercial trucks. Now there are many within a short distance from almost anywhere. This growth has served the commercial truck buyers and sellers alike.

It Can Be Lucrative

The commercial truck market can be very lucrative. One of the people I hired and trained started a commercial truck operation in a dealership in an old downtown location a couple miles from the freeway. He brought in a fully trained team and generated a million dollars gross in his operation the first year. His dealership went on to grow from there, leading to dramatic dealership expansion and a move to the auto mall at the freeway. These numbers do not even address the dramatic increases in service and parts and other areas within that dealership.

It is also a recession-resistant market, though it is not recession-proof. Having lived through several recessions while doing commercial trucks, typically where retail sales dropped as much as 50%, the commercial market remained flat or better. I've seen the commercial truck operation help a dealership through a tough economic period by maintaining sales and profits when their retail sales fell. I also must add that the recession period of 2007-11 was a different kind of recession which affected commercial trucks in a large way, while retail sales were also at all-time lows. That kind of period is certainly a challenge for all, and can be a real opportunity for those who remain committed to the commercial truck market. Why? During those times there are many dealerships that leave the commercial truck market, thus reducing competition. It is a natural weeding process!

New car and pickup truck profits have been going downhill for some time because anyone can find the cost of a new vehicle, the manufacturers have been reducing the markup for years, and new cars are very competitive in general. Many dealers I've seen are focused on their used vehicles allowing their new car franchise to legitimize their used vehicle operation. Since these used vehicles are highly profitable in comparison with new vehicles, they are willing to let new units go for less to keep the factory happy and their flooring down. So, it will be good news to know that the gross profits on new commercial trucks can be excellent! And, to top that off, the used commercial truck profits are huge!

The Goose That Lays the Golden Egg

I borrowed this phrase from one of my favorite mentors, Jim Rohn. He says that you just have to take care of and protect the goose that lays the golden egg. If you kill the goose that lays the golden egg, the game is over.

Throughout this book, everything I talk about when it comes to the operation of the Commercial Truck Department is intended to protect and enhance the dealer. I call the dealer the goose that lays the golden egg because it is the dealer that offers the real opportunity in the physical premises, funding, and leadership. All of my strategies and systems are meant to assist the dealer in understanding and accounting for their commercial operation, in addition to helping them be as profitable as possible.

Every decision I have made in the Commercial Truck Departments where I have been involved, whether as a manager or as a consultant, has been made with the dealer's best interests in mind. Protecting and enhancing the dealer is of paramount importance to me. I feel you have to watch out for the goose that lays the golden egg.

Let me state that this mindset about protecting and enhancing the dealer can lead some to be conservative and focus more on the protect part and less on the enhance part. That reminds me of Parable of the Talents from the Bible, with the one who went and buried the talent so it would be there when the owner returned. My idea is to focus more on the enhanced part because the dealer is already a risk taker by virtue of being in business and it is my job to be the person who doubled the talents, or acted aggressively. If I am to err, I will always err on the aggressive side rather than avoiding opportunity. I recommend this strategy for those who want to do well.

Within or Without, Part or Apart

Because of my philosophy of protecting and enhancing the dealer, I have developed strategies for integrating the Commercial Truck Department into the dealership as a whole. Whereas many dealerships allow it to be segregated, I prefer to have it fully integrated. Here is what I mean.

The One Person Band

Many dealerships will hire a person (usually one) to have them build a commercial truck or what many call a fleet or commercial/fleet department. Essentially this is one salesperson, which is sort of treated as a manager, but is in reality a salesperson. They might then allow this person to stock some upfitted commercial trucks and give them the authority to buy these on behalf of the dealership. All the while, the dealer and other managers above this person are not familiar with upfitted commercial trucks or the commercial truck market.

As a result of this, I have seen many times where this salesperson has ordered too many, or not a good mix, or has other problems with inventory. In addition, many times these salespeople can be compensated by the body companies to purchase units. In many, if not most of these cases, the dealer usually is unaware of that compensation. As a dealer, I would certainly be very interested in how my employee is being compensated to purchase product from vendors. I'm of the opinion that the dealer will almost always prefer a cost reduction rather than a cash incentive paid to employees. It's not the purchase incentive that is a problem. It is when the owner of the store is unaware of what is happening, that this presents a potential problem. If the owner approves it, then all is well.

Many of these salespeople hired to do this job may have income guarantees for a period of time to get the department rolling. Then when the guarantee is up and the inventory is in place, they may move on down the road leaving the dealer holding the bag.

I've seen dealers being left with as many as 60 upfitted trucks to deal with after a person left the store.

This is the dealer's fault in my opinion. He or she was a co-creator in this event by allowing it to be segregated in the first place, by not understanding the commercial truck market, and not following their own operation. This wouldn't happen on the retail side because the dealer is much more aware in that part of their operation.

To alleviate these kinds of situations, a Commercial Truck Department would serve the dealer more effectively by it being integrated into the whole operation. In this way, all the managers are aware, the dealer is aware, there is accountability, and it cannot get very far off track without the dealer noticing it.

This does not mean that it need be in the same building. But it does need to fit in the scheme of how the dealership and all its parts work together for the good of the whole.

Retail Integration

This is something I always talk about, but don't push very hard because there is disagreement between my philosophy and some dealers and even some manufacturers. However, I'm not one to buckle under that pressure because I learned this from experience and it has proven to be extremely effective and profitable.

It is this. Allow and even encourage the retail dealership staff to sell upfitted commercial trucks.

Many say that is not a good idea because they don't have the knowledge. I say that knowledge is easy to obtain through training. Many say that they will misrepresent the product due to their lack of knowledge and I say, if that is the case, I would advise getting rid of them immediately because they are likely doing that now.

For every objection that someone can possibly come up with on this, I can answer from experience. At the second commercial operation we had a fairly long-term retail staff.

I wanted my commercial guys out prospecting and not hugging their desk, as well as making it so that lot ups can be taken by qualified retail sales people. Consequently, I instituted training to all the retail staff and continued that for a long time. If they felt they were getting in trouble with answers to questions, they would come and ask, or come and get a commercial truck person to get involved. Otherwise, they would make the sale and all assistance would be given to do that.

As a result of this strategy, we were number one in a very wide regional, multi-state market and the only way that happened is because they sold almost 35% of all of the commercial trucks! Without that situation, my commercial people would have stayed at the dealership and sold less as well.

Keep in mind that a dealership with a revolving door for their retail staff creates a serious training challenge, but they also create a huge profit challenge to the dealership. In this scenario, offering the training to selected people on the staff might make more sense.

BUT, there's a critical instruction here.

If the retail staff is not trained they must not be allowed, under any circumstances, to sell a commercial truck. If a dealer allows a sale without the proper training and qualification of the salesperson, the Commercial Truck Department will become a failed operation in my opinion. It is so easy to misrepresent the product in commercial trucks. To say, 'I think that will carry about 5,000 lbs,' when in reality is has a capacity of 2,500 lbs can create a costly lawsuit. I've seen these kinds of lawsuits and they aren't fun.

To avoid training retail is not the answer. The answer is to train, train, and train. Ensure that only qualified people sell commercial trucks. The dealer is in charge of this philosophy and its integration.

One more reason to train. By training the retail staff to make them qualified to sell commercial trucks will increase your sales and your profits and be very beneficial to your operation.

The Team Concept

Our company promotes the team concept in Commercial Truck Departments. Putting one person in there and calling it a department is not as effective as having a team. It will produce minimal to very modest results at best. We need a team. The team need not be large in numbers to begin with, but it must be a team to be effective.

If, on the retail side, you put one salesperson out there and had him or her be their own manager you would have a similar situation to what many dealers think will produce different results in a commercial truck operation.

Dealers have a team on the retail side. They need one on the commercial side, too. On the retail side there is a manager and salespeople, or a manager, closers, and liners, or whatever system structure they may have. But in all of them it is a team of people designed to get the best results over time.

For the commercial operation a team is needed as well. This can begin with a manager and a salesperson as an absolute minimum, but would be best served by also having an administrative assistant. In fact, I think this administrative assistant is a key person in this operation. To me, this is a must have. This team will be effective by having different people doing different jobs all focused on the objective of growth.

In addition, this method has the potential for substantial growth. With only one person a dealership is automatically limited to that one person's capacities and expertise.

Why the Team?

Besides the obvious of not being limited to what only one person can do in a day, week, month, or year, the biggest reason for a team is that the commercial truck operation should be, in my opinion, a prospecting organization. In other words, it is their job to bring in business that would likely have not come in to the dealership otherwise. This means that we have a salesperson that is essentially considered an "outside" salesperson—meaning they go outside and bring business in.

Auto dealerships generally do not understand the idea of an outside salesperson, have never managed that position, and have no systems or strategies to do so. I have seen so many of them attempt to do it and fail at it, then say that stuff doesn't work, and quit doing it. The reality is they didn't know how and/or didn't want to learn, or were not sufficiently involved.

Since this isn't understood very well on the retail side, we need a manager on the commercial side who understands it. The salesperson then would be scheduled to do outside prospecting on a *daily basis* for a couple hours a day minimum. The manager would train and manage this procedure with the assistance of the administrative assistant. In times when the manager needs to physically go out with the salesperson, the administrative assistant can take care of the phone and general needs of the operation in their absence.

As the department expands, additional salespeople would be added to grow the department further. In the beginning we need only start with a small team. With this team, it can expand from this small team to a large team very easily and efficiently because the systems, procedures, and individual duties would be the same. However, if you had one person and wanted to expand, that would not have the same kind of results. You would still not have a team, but only two sales people. So, starting with this small team of manager, sales person, and administrative assistant has many benefits and has a much greater opportunity for success.

Prospecting vs. Waiting for "Ups"

Going out prospecting requires a plan and a commitment. I've seen so many dealerships who have tried it unsuccessfully. Their salesperson will go out for a few days. One person they talked to while prospecting will come into the store and buy a vehicle. Another sales person will get the commission stating that the prospect didn't ask for them. It usually only takes that to happen once and the prospecting stops. There needs to be a better plan than this.

Other times, I've seen a dealership's commercial department hire someone, send them out with little or no supervision or training, and pay a guarantee for 60 to 90 days. When the guarantee runs out, the employee does, too. That ends the prospecting idea. I hear, "That stuff doesn't work," so often. What it should be is "I failed to plan, train, follow up, and follow through and this plan failed as a result of my poor efforts and strategy."

Prospecting works if it is worked and managed and it doesn't when it isn't. It's that simple. Prospecting is not a magic bullet. It is a legitimate and productive tool if it is managed well.

Remember, the benefit of the prospecting is to bring business in to the dealership that is not coming in now. When this is done successfully, it is the most effective advertising the dealership can do. Yet many dealerships will spend all kinds of money on newspaper ads and aren't willing to invest in salaries for effective prospectors. It's all a mindset. If you want it to work, it will work. If you want it to fail, it will.

Doodling vs. Professional Drawing

Doodling is drawing, but it is ineffective, limited drawing. I see many commercial truck operations doodling. It's as if they aren't serious about what they do and they are always ineffective in my experience. They may commit to the inventory and may even carry a larger number than I would advise (hard to believe, but true!). But their doodling mentality keeps them from success.

Opening a store and putting inventory out is the easiest thing in the world, but it is just a part of being successful at running a profitable store. In addition, it can put a store out of business in a hurry with excessive flooring charges.

The doodling mentality permeates the organization. It isn't just the inventory. That is only one part. The paperwork, the lack of tracking numbers, equipment, and the list goes on-and-on. If we are to have the best chance at success, it must be a professional operation that is serious about long-term success.

Long-Term vs. Short-Term

"I think I'll try it for a few months" is a death knell. Might as well not try at all, I say. The only success will be with a long-term attitude—a commitment to its success. I like the phrase from the Apollo 13 mission, "failure is not an option." That is commitment.

In my travels seeing a few hundred dealerships, I can see the long-term or short-term thinking played out visually. It is demonstrated in the inventory, where the inventory is displayed, how it is displayed, the equipment used in the operation, the Service Department, the attitude of people associated and not associated with the commercial truck operation, and more.

As an example of short-term thinking, I've worked at dealerships that won't buy business cards for a salesperson until after they've been there more than ninety days. For as little as business cards cost, this is a travesty. But more than this, it is a commitment to failure. Success can only happen by overcoming the dealership's own resistance.

Goals

When consulting, one of the first questions Commercial Truck Success invariably asks a dealer is, "What would you like this operation to add to your overall operation in terms of income and sales?" Sometimes, I say point blank, "What do you want this operation to do for you?" I want to see where their mind is in terms of what they want or expect. Some have rather modest goals and others are very aggressive. It doesn't matter what they are to me, but it matters very much how the operation will be built and managed. In any case, we design our consulting to match the dealer's goals.

The goal or vision should not be underplayed here. It is critical to the successful outcome. How a person sees what they want and what the potential is has everything to do with what they are willing to do to see it become a reality.

Fleet vs. Commercial

My first opportunity at doing commercial trucks came at a dealership that had started what they called a Commercial Accounts Department. They put a trailer way over in the back corner of their lot with a selling manager and a couple of sales people. The manager made most of the sales, selling against the sales people. They didn't really do anything commercial, it was touted to be business sales to companies and organizations. The manager left unexpectedly, the department was in a death spiral, and I was asked to go in and turn it around.

I assessed the department and what they did. To me it was tantamount to taking money out of one pocket, throwing some on the ground, putting the rest in the other pocket, and calling it a profit. Basically what they did was cheap sell popular products, and in reality, they were decreasing overall profits with that strategy. This, I was to learn, was a rather typical strategy for commercial truck operations that called themselves a fleet department or commercial/fleet. In reality they were doing very little of either, mostly selling retail at a lower price and profit.

Because of my 'think like an aggressive dealer' mentality, I thought this was ineffective to say the least. I thought about what could be done to change it and decided to stock upfitted commercial trucks. That became the Commercial Truck Department and we began selling units the dealership was not currently selling. Any sales in this arena became additional profits and sales, rather than the same sales for less.

Many dealerships have a fleet department, but it is in name only. It is rare that they actually sell to true fleet customers. Usually they sell a few to local political subdivisions such as a city or county, but the rest of their sales or the majority of them are to retail buyers.

I also know of several dealerships that truly have a serious fleet department selling large numbers of legitimate fleet vehicles to legitimate fleet buyers. Their profitable department is a testimony to their success.

The commercial truck market is essentially a retail market in my opinion and experience, and it most often has equal or greater profits than a normal retail sale. It is not a fleet market. Though commercial trucks are sold to legitimate fleet users, the vast majority of commercial trucks are sold to small business, which is a retail market. Many fleet/commercial departments don't understand that difference and the result of that lack of understanding is lower gross profits.

True fleet is about the most competitive arena in vehicle sales. The margins are often so small, that a minor mistake in quoting can lead to major losses. It is a market that requires a studied expertise and keen awareness, and it is certainly not for most dealerships to entertain and be profitable at. Cash flow can be a nightmare for those not knowledgeable and it can even be a nightmare for those who are. Yes, it can be very profitable. A clear focus with a long-term commitment is required.

The most common commercial truck is sold to a company that has less than ten units, and many have less than five in their 'fleet'. They are contractors, vendors, service companies, and more. They deliver flowers, auto parts, boxes of stuff, glass, and more. They carry parts, tools, and machines to do work on the jobsite. The majority are small businesses and not fleet users.

I've seen many commercial/fleet sales people put $500 or less profit in a deal when they could have had $2,500.

It becomes a mindset. You think it is an ultra-competitive fleet market and choose to be ultra-conservative. As a result, many Commercial Truck Departments that I have seen are not really profitable at all and often are a drain on profits.

Now, this being said, in order for the commercial truck market to be the most profitable, it needs to be long-term and this requires a different 'dealership experience' than is typical in many stores. These customers need to be treated a bit differently, more like business people. They will pay the money and they will be happy with it as well. They want to be treated with respect, courtesy, ease, and speed.

Of course, my recommendation is that every customer in the dealership be treated this way.

One Price Strategy

In my own operations, I adopted a one price selling strategy of units in stock that worked extremely well for us. I priced units with gross profit and also a meaningful discount to demonstrate to the commercial buyer our fairness in pricing. The customers seemed to like this approach as well and it was easy enough to explain to them.

Of course, it didn't work every time, but most of the time it worked great. In addition, it really helped where the sales people were concerned and we held larger gross profits in my opinion that would have been otherwise.

We began this at my first operation and continued it throughout. We also used it with very similar results with all of the dealers where we have consulted.

It's a Whole New Market

The commercial truck market is a whole new market to a dealer not currently in this market. I liken it to a dealer who only sells cars and now sells cars and pickup trucks, too. Adding the pickup truck line adds a whole new market to their existing operation. Adding commercial upfitted trucks to a dealership that has cars and pickups will be the same kind of addition. It's going to be a whole new market for them.

It's a Regional Market

The commercial truck market is a regional market rather than a local market. Companies will do business farther away to have the relationship they want and need and to get the trucks they need in their business. Regularly we used to deliver units 500 miles away from our dealership. Overall it's not necessarily that wide of a region, but it covers a somewhat greater area than is typical in a dealer's market area.

75/25

In addition to that, selling a commercial truck is a door-opening opportunity to the buying power of the business employees, owners, and managers.

Here's something you might find very interesting. In my educated opinion and experience, commercial upfitted truck sales in a very successful commercial truck operation within a retail dealership will only be about 25% of sales on average. This means that 75% of their sales come from the products you already sell. *There are several reasons for this:*

One, is because it is a prospecting organization. There is an opportunity to make sales to employees of companies, company managers, and owners because they don't drive commercial trucks for personal use. Think about the average number of employees at a company and the fact that they all drive something, and probably have more than one in their own personal 'fleet'.

Two, by virtue of the fact that it is commercial trucks the dealership sells, we can legitimately approach businesses on a B2B, or Business To Business level. This is more readily accepted by the businesses contacted and easier and more effective for the dealership as prospectors and sellers.

Three, it is the commercial truck operation's best strategy to expand sales across the board. Commercial trucks are only a part of what we have to sell. We want to sell our Service Department, parts, used vehicles, and more. In other words, it is our job to tell the whole story, not just part of it.

Fourth, sales are all about relationships. As we prospect effectively, make sales, do business in service, and so on, we are developing a relationship with the company and its people. A natural extension of that relationship is getting the customer more comfortable with our dealership. Consequently, many of these sales are sales that would likely not have been made by our dealership utilizing their standard business attraction methods.

If I see an operation where they are selling a really high percentage of commercial trucks in their total sales,

I see money left on the table in a big way. They are missing all those opportunities of sales to business employees and managers.

The best reasons to get involved in the commercial truck market are to increase your sales and profits, understand that market is a retail market, know it is a whole new market, and to realize it is a highly profitable market. If done well, about seventy-five percent of sales will be of product you already stock and sell, including used vehicles.

In addition to the sales, the dealership will benefit dramatically by the service business generated when going after the commercial truck market, including use by employees of those businesses.

Service, Parts, and Body Shop

One of the biggest benefactors of a commercial truck operation is the Service Department, Parts Department, and Body Shop. Often, in building a commercial truck operation, getting people in for service comes before a sale. It only makes sense. People don't need a new vehicle as regularly as they need an oil change or other service. By getting them in for service, we have the opportunity to build a better relationship with that person or company which can lead to sales when that need exists.

An aggressive Service and Parts Department can really go after this market in a big way and expand their overall operation dramatically. This can be one of the most profitable areas when adding a commercial truck operation to the dealership. I've also seen a few dealers who were aggressive in service and less so in sales. Those dealers built a large Commercial Service Department while only a modest Commercial Sales Department.

The other more important aspect of this is that commercial users use their vehicles commercially. In other words, it's not an option. They use their vehicle for their livelihood, so when that vehicle needs repair, time is of the essence. An aggressive commercial service operation will find many ways to serve this market and create strong relationships with those clients by offering a pick-up and delivery service, late service hours, and many other creative ideas.

Finding Good People

Finding good people is always a challenge. I will go into various ways of finding people for the Commercial Truck Department which can also be used on the retail side.

Commercial Inventory

This is a scary thing for a lot of dealers because they don't understand it. They think it is so very different from their retail inventory…but in reality it is not that different.

The first question I usually get is "How many do I have to have?" I have developed a plan from experience that is effective and I will go into detail in the Inventory Chapter. However, each is a reasonable number that makes sense within a dealership's overall inventory levels.

The Mix

The inventory mix is critical. Another reason there needs to be a certain number in stock is because there are many different bodies and applications. I've seen dealers who stocked too many of one thing and not enough variety. I will go into great detail in the Inventory Chapter about this subject.

Turning Inventory and Inventory Costs

Turning inventory is something all dealers understand. Turning commercial inventory is just as important as retail inventory, however it is a slightly different animal in that commercial inventory may turn a bit slower on average. This should not diminish the profitability. Many manufacturers offer additional flooring reimbursement for stocking upfitted trucks, so that can offset part of this flooring expense. In addition, on many units the profits can be somewhat greater than average unit profits, again offsetting expenses nicely.

Other issues that affect the turning of commercial inventory can be having a good mix, making sure everything is ready to sell, and inventory looking good. I've seen a lot of dealers who ignore the upkeep of commercial units but wash the retail units regularly. Inventory is inventory and we want them ready to be delivered immediately—or as close to that as possible.

Display may also have a role in turning commercial inventory. Having the inventory where it can be seen can make a difference.

I will go into much more detail about inventory and all the issues surrounding it in the Inventory Chapter. The main thing I want to impart here in the overview is the need to stock the inventory and to treat it similarly to retail inventory as in maintaining it, having a good mix, and so on.

Training for Commercial

I believe very strongly in good training. In commercial, far more than in retail, there is a good deal of knowledge that is key to making the department a success. There is so much more than just knowing the options, colors, and models.

Because a commercial truck can be overloaded and people can be injured as a result of this, it is important to know what body is right for which chassis, how people load different bodies, center of gravity issues, understanding trailering in commercial trucks, and so on. Some of this knowledge can come from the manufacturer's training just like the retail training. Additional training can be from body companies and others who have specific training programs designed just for this market.

As stated earlier, I also believe it is important to offer training to the retail staff as well if they are interested, or if the dealership is interested in promoting this. If the dealership is also willing to introduce the retail staff to the commercial market and allow them to become 'authorized sellers' of commercial trucks it makes for more of a well-rounded dealership.

Marketing Strategies

For the commercial truck operation, we will need a specific budget to take advantage of marketing opportunities. Based on what that budget is, we recommend how that can be spent effectively.

The main marketing strategy is prospecting. This means salaries plus commission and not commission only. The word 'salary' is a problem with many dealerships when it comes to their sales organizations. However ... trust me on this from experience. It makes all the difference in success. This allows us to control the prospecting and not just expect it or hope for it. Think of it as advertising expense if you must, and that is essentially a good way to view it.

As part of the prospecting marketing strategy, securing a good downloadable list is also critical.

In my first operation I bought a good downloadable truck user database list. It was from Dun & Bradstreet® and they called it the TRINC list. This proved to be the single most effective thing I did. Back in late 1989 and early 1990, I ended up spending $10,000 for the complete list purchased in segments. It was approximately a 10,000 name database. Our profit from that list made the amount spent seem insignificant, yet at the time the dealer thought it was expensive. For this reason, I bought it in pieces until I had the whole geographical span I wanted. I focused on the county we were in, all the counties that surrounded and touched ours, plus one more that was very close. This proved to be a great strategy.

Traditional forms of advertising will take a back seat to other kinds of marketing such as having a separate website, blog, social media, newsletter, and so on. The new way to market via the Internet has proven to be extremely effective if done with this multi-faceted strategy.

If there is money left over, then I would choose publications that cater to the commercial truck market, such as the Commercial Truck Trader and other such publications.

Other marketing strategies include networking, Chamber of Commerce mixers, service clubs, referral clubs, and so on. These can be very effective in the long term.

I will go into much more detail about marketing strategies in the Marketing Strategies Chapter.

That's the overview ... now let's get to more specifics in each chapter.

CHAPTER Two

INVENTORY

Truck Classifications

Trucks are classified by the GVWR or Gross Vehicle Weight Rating determined by the manufacturer. *Here is a list of classes:*

Class 1 has a GVWR range of 0-6,000 lbs. This includes cars and 1/2-ton pickups.

Class 2a has a GVWR range of 6,001 to 8,500 lbs. This includes 1/2-ton and some 3/4-ton pickups.

Class 2b has a GVWR range of 8,501 to 10,000 lbs. This includes most 3/4-ton and many 1-ton pickups and cab chassis.

Class 3 has a GVWR range of 10,001 to 14,000 lbs. This includes most 1-ton cab chassis.

Class 4 has a GVWR range of 14,001 to 16,000 lbs. This includes most HD 1-ton models like 4500 or 450.

Class 5 has a GVWR range of 16,001 to 19,500 lbs. This includes most HD 1-ton models like 4500, 450 and the 5500 and 550 type vehicles.

Class 6 has a GVWR range of 19,501 to 26,000 lbs. This includes medium duty trucks like the *Ford* F650.

Class 7 has a GVWR range of 26,001 to 33,000 lbs. This includes medium duty trucks like the *Ford* F750. It is also the threshold where a Commercial Driver's License is required.

Class 8 is GVWR 33,001 and greater. This included Heavy Duty trucks, tractor trailers and such.

For the purposes of this book and our focus, we are concerned with classes 1-7. Class 8 is a different market entirely. Class 7 is a limited market that we won't get very involved in. Classes 1-3 is the largest market by far, and this will be our largest focus. Classes 4 and 5 are large markets for HD truck users and are very profitable.

Chassis Types

There are three basic chassis types that we will discuss.

Conventional Cab

This cab chassis looks a lot like a pickup in the front, although in the heavier duty models including medium duty, that cab may be larger. Essentially, you sit behind the front wheels with the engine in front of you. This is the most common cab chassis by far. Almost all truck manufacturers make conventional cab chassis models. These cover class 1 through class 8.

Cutaway Chassis

This cab chassis looks a lot like a Van Body in the front. It is a Van Body where the body has been cut away behind the driver to accommodate a body application. They began by installing van bodies, but now many different body types are available on this unit. The engine is partially in front of you and also partly between you and the passenger in that the rear of the engine intrudes a bit into the cabin. The advantage of this unit is a shorter turning radius and shorter overall length. These chassis are almost all class 2b and 3 and manufactured by *Ford, GM* and *RAM* predominantly.

Tilt-Cab Chassis

This cab chassis has the cab mounted directly over the engine, so the driver sits higher than in the other chassis types. In addition, rather than a hood that opens, the cab tilts to expose the engine area. The advantage of this unit is an extremely short turning radius, shorter overall length, and much more. These are normally class 3 through 7 trucks. Isuzu is the largest manufacturer of this type of chassis. Other popular brands are *UD (Nissan), Hino (Toyota), Fuso (Mitsubishi)*.

Stocking Upfitted Trucks

An upfitted truck is a cab chassis with a body mounted on it. It can be a Service or Utility Body, Flatbed, Dump Body, you name it. It is NOT an empty cab chassis.

To an auto dealer, stocking inventory is a given. Yet when it comes to commercial inventory, many dealers I have seen want to take a different path. Commercial trucks are not for the timid. However, it doesn't require a lot of courage either. What it requires is a desire, number one. And two, it requires an understanding of this market through knowledge.

Stocking upfitted, ready to go to work truck inventory is a requirement to success in this market. The main reason for that is the same as stocking on the retail side. People want what they want as soon as they can get it. Having it available right now, this minute, aids the buyer as much as the dealer. In fact, it might even be more important on the commercial side. Because in my experience, contractors wait until they needed it two weeks ago and then want it yesterday. It is not an elective purchase, it is based on need. Their business depends on it.

Cab Chassis vs. Upfitted Truck

I understand the reasoning on the empty chassis stocking. Many times a dealer thinks there are so many different bodies they could put on that chassis. So if they choose one, they're stuck and might lose a sale. I guarantee they would have lost far more sales by stocking empty chassis than making body choices. People want to buy a completed unit. They want to see a truck already built. Those that want something very special realize and understand they will not ever find it in stock and they are willing to wait, but they are a very small portion of the market.

In addition to this, an empty cab chassis is an incomplete vehicle. It is not salable as is and cannot be registered (at least in California) until it has been completed by having a body installed and a weight certificate issued.

Here's the main reason to stock upfitted trucks: much larger profits. The second main reason is that contractors in general wait until they needed it two weeks ago and then want it yesterday. Maybe they had an engine blow, or a crash, or some other thing that created the immediate need. The key word here is immediate.

The main reason about increased profit is that it is tied to the need. Anyone can sell an empty chassis cheap and have a body installed in three to six weeks. Consequently, via the idea of competition, many dealers would then compete over the lowest gross profit and sell for less. In addition, there would be more dealers in the commercial market because of the lack of risk and investment.

If you have one built and ready, you can command a greater price even though another dealer is trying to cheap sell their chassis. The reason is that the customer needs it now. I ask the client, "How much money do you make per day?" "How much will waiting three to six weeks cost you in dollars?" "Look how much you are saving right now by having this unit today—not even considering the jobs you can't complete because you don't have the truck you need."

Previously I said that I became number one in my market and even a wide multi-state regional market. I can assure you that this would not have been possible by stocking empty chassis.

Hence, the reason for this chapter and the detail in this chapter is to help understand commercial upfitted inventory as much as possible. Plus, I want to alleviate fear and to increase confidence and success in this market for you.

First, if a dealer is unwilling to stock upfitted commercial trucks, but says they want a successful commercial operation, I strongly suggest they get out now or don't ever get involved in the commercial market. It will be a waste of time and money. Focus on what you do best and forget about commercial trucks.

Now that we have that out of the way, let's learn about stocking commercial upfitted trucks.

You've Come to the Right Place

Well ... one of them, anyway. Commercial truck inventory is one of my favorite subjects. I love commercial trucks, have experimented greatly, and made plenty of mistakes along with many more successes. I'm sure that I could write an entire book about this subject, but I will endeavor to keep it succinct, yet thorough.

How Many?

One question I've found on almost every dealer's mind who wants to get into the commercial market is "How many do I need to stock?" It's a good question.

I've developed a practical formula to help a dealer put it into perspective with the rest of their operation. It is this: stock 15% of your total new and used average monthly sales to begin with. So, if a dealer is averaging 100 new and used units in an average month, he would stock 15 upfitted commercial trucks. This works very well to get a dealer started in the commercial market.

The second question is usually, "How many of those need to have bodies?" The answer is: all of them. If you want to stock a couple empty chassis, then add them to the number. It is 15 upfitted trucks. Cargo vans are not upfitted trucks, although they could have a bin package in them. Those would be added to the mix as well, but not part of the 15%.

The reasons for this are many. **One,** this number puts this operation in perspective within the dealership inventory as a significant portion. **Two,** it allows a dealer to stock a reasonable mix of bodies to help satisfy and encourage the market. **Three,** it demonstrates a commitment to the market. This is important for the dealer as well as a demonstration to potential clients that you are serious about this market and not just doodling.

I cannot emphasize enough that a willingness to stock the inventory **_and_** understand the commercial inventory is critical to success.

What Should I Stock?

That's a great question. It will probably be a bit different in Albany, New York than in San Diego, California or Billings, Montana, or Oklahoma City, Oklahoma. But not a lot different. There are regional differences for sure, but the basic body choices are going to apply universally. The main difference will be the mix and some slight differences. For example in the southern states, they sell a serious number of gooseneck style steel and aluminum Flatbeds for ranchers and 'wanna be' ranchers. In California where I live, that is saleable, but not popular in comparison. In the snow regions of the country, steel, aluminum, and stainless steel dump bodies sell in large quantity, yet in California it is a stockable, but slower moving unit.

I am confident that I could go anywhere in the country, regardless of the size of the city and create a successful commercial truck operation. This is how I would start:

I would sit by several different higher traffic areas, such as freeway, major highway, etc. and record what I see in the way of commercial upfitted trucks, along with cargo vans and pickups—especially pickups with racks. I would make columns like in a spreadsheet and then just make a hash mark each time I see one. Even in a very high traffic area, I can record them accurately with this method. I would spend about a week doing this at various times of the day and record each day or different locations on a different sheet. Then, I would compile and sort the information to tell me the mix and the size of the mix that I saw. Don't forget to make note of colored commercial trucks—the ones that aren't white. That will be important.

My columns would be something like this: Service Body SRW (Single Rear Wheel) Regular Cab, Service Body SRW Extended or Crew Cab, Service Body Regular Cab DRW (Dual Rear Wheel), Service Body Extended Cab or Crew Cab DRW, Service Body with Crane. Consider also how many have racks, how many have cargo area enclosures, raised roofs, and so on. Look at the features to see options to stock and sell. I would include Flatbed SRW, Flatbed DRW, how many have Stakeside Gates, any with Cranes, then Gooseneck Bodies SRW, Gooseneck DRW, Steel Dump Bodies, Van Bodies on Cutaway Chassis, Van Bodies on other chassis, and so on.

The main thing is to record as much information as possible to know what is being used currently or at least on those days in your area. This will be your basic market, so stocking to match that will help get you off to a good start. Initially, I suggest stocking about 75% of your stock that matches your regional market. The other 25% will be for experimentation in stocking what you think this market can use. In other words, solutions they may not have seen or thought of to help the client do their job better or more efficiently.

Color vs. White

Conservative dealers will stock only white and they will always stay conservative as a result. When you are checking your market by watching traffic, I have no doubt that you will see a substantial number of colored trucks. This is the market that few commercial dealers are courageous enough to take advantage of, but I can assure you that it is sizeable.

In my second commercial operation after being convinced to stock colored upfitted trucks at the first operation, I expanded my colored truck stocking to as high as 40% of my entire inventory. Now, I wouldn't advise any dealer starting out to be that bold unless boldness is part of their nature. But, I would advise dealers to stock colored units from the beginning in smaller quantities. I can tell you that I think this was one of the major keys to my success. I had zero competition. And, guess what? I sold them all at significant profits.

Don't be afraid of color. Start with the safer colors. Red is a very safe color, black is also pretty safe. Start there.

Up Level vs. Strippy

Some dealers might think the commercial truck market drives only stripped-down trucks with vinyl seats. Wrong. The vast majority in California have cloth seats (they breathe!), air conditioning, tilt steering wheel, stereo radios, CD players, and so on. You will even find several with power windows and door locks, up level trim packages, and more.

Some of your stock should cater to the general contractor types who don't have big crews because they sublet their work when needed, but they like their comfort going from job to job and bid to bid. They might want a Service Body to carry tools with them, but they like their power windows and their up level super comfortable seats—maybe even, power seats.

You will find that these units sell and they sell for higher profits.

Truck Body Options

There are standard bodies and then there are the bodies with options. Just as with retail inventory, a basic unit will bring a below average gross profit and a loaded unit a much higher gross profit typically. The same thing applies in commercial trucks. Remember, it is a retail market.

In stocking Service or Utility Bodies, there are a lot of options to make it more useful. Some of them include a cargo area enclosure, master locking system, power locks, BedSlide, drawers, lighting for night work, transverse compartments, different height compartments, a material rack, a stand up inside roof enclosure, and more. In order to demonstrate the usefulness of these kinds of options, it is important to have some of them on your stock units.

Each manufacturer has a list of options. It would be good to become familiar with them and demonstrate them to your clients.

Truck body options is an area where I have had huge success in and so little competition. I am all about solutions and by stocking a lot of options, I can show clients ways to save them money, save their back, help them be more efficient, carry more things effectively, and much more. Where almost all the dealers within 200 miles of me stocked plain bodies with maybe a rack and a hitch, I would stock ones with cargo bed enclosures, power locks, and many other options. It is just amazing how beneficial this can be to create sales—and more important, create loyal customers.

In fact, when working for the truck body company, I sold dealers a lot of options to help them make more sales because of my experience in that market. This benefitted the body company, the dealer, and the end user alike.

Securing Inventory

There are numerous ways to get inventory. You can order empty cab chassis units from the factory, then take them or drop ship them to a selected body company to have the body installed. Another way that has become the number one way for *Chevy, GMC, Ford,* and *RAM* dealers to get inventory is to use the bailment pool system that those manufacturers have set up.

A bailment pool is typically a body upfitter or manufacturer who agrees to stock empty cab chassis for dealers to pull from while then upfitting the chassis with a body they sell. This arrangement is for the benefit of the dealer, the manufacturer, and the end user alike and the main benefit is speed. If the chassis is already built and at the body company, then the six to eight week period of getting the chassis is alleviated.

These bailment pool dealers operate by the same kind of rules regarding that inventory as any dealer in that they pay flooring expenses if the unit doesn't move within a specified period of time. This creates a strong desire on the behalf of the body company to move the unit. This sometimes creates incentives which can benefit everyone.

When a unit is ordered out of the bailment system, it is invoiced to the dealer just as if they ordered it directly from the factory to begin with. In fact, the body company or manufacturer cannot sell the vehicle to anyone other than a dealer, so they are non-competitive. The bailment pool body company typically doesn't make any money on the chassis. Their money is earned from the body installed on the chassis and having the chassis in stock to help dealers creates more business for the body company than they might normally have. The body is invoiced separately from the chassis.

The bailment system is a very efficient and effective way to secure inventory for stock and to satisfy sold orders for specialty pieces when needed. It saves time and money for everyone generally.

Another way to get inventory is to buy it from another stocking dealer. This can be an advantage in getting upfitted units within a day or two rather than weeks. It can also be a huge opportunity that I will address later in the book.

Many times the factory competes with their own bailment system. In this situation, we have a retail factory representative trying to get orders through the normal retail ordering system to make their quota though a dealer may prefer to deal with the bailment pool system which comes through a fleet allocation system. Each dealer needs to choose how they will deal with this, but my experience is that going through the bailment system is generally the best bet. The main reason this competition exists is that the factory needs to keep moving and the bailment units were built some time ago and they are trying to fill production lines now or in the near future.

How Units Are Equipped

The options on the cab chassis you stock are important. When ordering from the factory, you can obviously order anything you might want, but the bailment system is different. In the bailment system, each individual body company orders the units in mix of models and option content for their individual pool. They try to stock what they think people want so that they turn their inventory as quickly as possible.

An aggressive dealer or one with an individual market strategy may want options that the bailment system doesn't normally stock. This can be negotiated with each body company as desired. Many of them will be willing to stock units specifically for your dealership providing you take them before they have to pay flooring interest on them. That is fair for everyone.

As an example of what I'm talking about, as a *Chevy* dealer stocking upfitted trucks, I ordered the wide rear axle option on every unit I could. It looked better, lowered the center of gravity, and was an inexpensive option. Most dealers didn't even think about it, but I used it as a selling feature. I would ask my favorite bailment pool companies to stock units with this and other options that I felt would set me apart with my customers. Some of those options might be locking differential or limited slip axle, tilt steering wheel so that it accommodates different size drivers comfortably and safely, engine hour meter, up level radios, up level trim, colored units, and so on.

This helped me a great deal and I know it will help anyone who desires to follow suit.

Choosing Bailment Pool and Body Company Partners

Some commercial operations like to spread their business around widely taking advantage of specials when they exist and generally focusing on price. I choose partners. Price is way down the list. This strategy has been extremely effective for me and for those I have taught this strategy.

When I first began in the commercial market, I found an excellent body company. This was a small company, but aggressive, and this was before the bailment system was widespread. Though they didn't have a bailment pool, I sent them so much business that they became almost exclusive with me. We were like partners. They helped me in so many ways and by virtue of that assistance, they got my business.

It worked really well for a time. Then, the two brothers who owned it decided to not do that business any more, and within a few weeks were gone.

I had to start all over.

This time, I went in search of a few key partners. I went to their operations and interviewed them, told them what I was doing, what I wanted in the way of a body company partner, and so on. From that point on, I have used this system with the best results.

Here are a few reasons to choose a partner rather than just buy on price from whoever is having the deal of the week.

When you choose a partner that you give a good deal of business to, by virtue of that commitment to them, you can make requests for service and pricing that they would not normally be interested in doing. By you helping them, helping you is a given. The more business is given, the more important the partnership.

Nobody gets more than 50%. Under no circumstances will I give more than 50% of my business to one company. I learned that lesson really well. However, I am going to choose three or four companies to give most of my business.

As a result of this partnering approach, the bailment pool company will be more open to stocking units the way you want them, and to giving you preferential treatment in production. This can be a huge benefit for certain customers. They will also be willing and encouraged to stock more of the kind of bodies that you normally order so you can get units very quickly in comparison with the norm.

Depending on the volume you give these body companies, they will be interested when encouraged to assist you in marketing, stocking incentives, low cost body swaps, and much more.

Because of the volume of business that you have with a few, there is much more interest in you as a dealer. This means more attention is paid to your account, you hear about new things quicker, special offers are a natural event, and much more.

You could try to play one against the other, but that wouldn't be beneficial in my mind. Keep all dealings straightforward and above board and it will work out very, very well.

In other words, they really are a partner in your success. Treating them in that manner and giving them a good portion of your business demonstrates that you are also that partner to them. It is mutually beneficial, as it should be. In fact, it has been my experience to use this method across the board in life. I partner with people instead of trying to have an advantage on them and we all win.

Consignment Units

Some body companies may offer to give units on consignment. I am not a fan of consignment and it is ineffective in my experience. There are always exceptions to any rules, so make your own choice. However, as a general rule, body companies are not interested in consignment and it is not a good deal for them. Think partnership. Each should benefit. For one to benefit and not the other is not a good deal.

The other thing about consignment is that it will dramatically limit what you will be able to stock and achieve because very few offer it. Those that do are usually trying to unload an old unit they haven't been able to sell. Consignment is generally a bad deal.

Here's a better suggestion than consignment. If they have an old unit and you think it is a saleable piece that you could make some money on, make them an offer at a super bargain price to cash them out of it. If they accept, you have a serious bargain and they have recovered some of their investment. This way, you can both move on instead of having to continue to deal with this inventory issue. I have used this for advantage and profitability many times.

Commercial Truck Body Types

Basically, there are three types of basic bodies. There is a Service or Utility Body, a Flatbed, and a Van Body. Pretty much, most truck bodies are some kind of modification of these three basic foundations.

There are hundreds of variations on these popular bodies, but here is a listing of popular standard bodies that I see throughout the country.

Service or Utility Body

Some people call it a Service Body and others call it a Utility Body and they are normally referring to the same thing. Generally, this is a steel body with compartments and doors for holding tools, parts, etc. for people to use as they work at jobsites. They come in different lengths and widths depending on the chassis they are mounted on. The most popular lengths are 8-, 9- and 11-feet. In California, this is the most popular body and rightly so. It is useful for so many varied businesses. The compartments have doors that lock and shelves that adjust so a wide variety of things can be carried from job to job. They usually have open top lids which allow small parts to be carried.

There are lots of options and modifications of this basic body. The USC Combo Body is a modification of the Service Body where it is a Service Body with the last compartment cut off and a platform extension of the floor made to be used as a work platform. The enclosed Service Body, sometimes called a plumbers body because plumbers love it, is basically a Service Body with a raised roof. There are numerous modifications of a Service Body. They are also not just limited to steel bodies. Service Bodies are available in aluminum, fiberglass, or composite materials.

Flatbed/Stakebed

This is just a flat floor body that carries things from one place to another. It can be loaded with pallets, hay, boxes, you name it. It's a drayage vehicle. You can have different floor materials like wood, smooth or diamond plate steel, wood and steel for more strength, or composite materials. Popular options include stakeside gates, hitch, material rack, tapered headboard, tool boxes, and much more. It is a very popular basic body.

Gooseneck or 5th Wheel Body

This is a morph of the Flatbed where it has a gooseneck or 5th wheel hitch installed in the middle of the bed directly over the rear axle for hauling heavy trailers such as horse trailers, commercial dumping trailers, and such. It is usually slightly shorter to accommodate the trailer turn angle so that the trailer doesn't hit the tail end of the bed. These are available in steel *(usually diamond plate steel is the most common)*, aluminum, and composite materials.

Contractor Body

In California and surrounding states, this is a modification of a Flatbed and it combines some of the virtues of a Service Body and a Flatbed. It has become a standard product of many manufacturers with these typical features in a package: tapered headboard, upper body tool boxes with fold-down doors and open top lids (like a Service Body), under body tool boxes, short 'contractor style' gates around the rear with a load divider board at the back of the upper bed tool boxes, a tapered HD rack (usually forklift loadable), and a class IV receiver and trailer plug.

You can see why the Contractor Body can be popular in that it combines tool boxes of various types with the usefulness of the Flatbed, rack, and gates. It is used by a wide variety of contractors—hence the name 'Contractor Body.'

In other parts of the country a Contractor Body is often a steel dump with split fold-down sides and sometimes other types of bodies.

Plumber Style Body

This has specific names depending on the manufacturer. As an example, Knapheide calls theirs a KUV, Harbor Truck Bodies calls theirs a WorkMaster, and so on.

Essentially this unit is a modified Service Body in that a roof is added that may be cab height, or high enough to be able to stand up in it.

It is useful in that you can carry tools and small parts and things to jobs and also carry larger items inside the roof section of the body and keep them out of sight and secure while parked. Inside the roof section are shelves for more parts, tools and in the center area secure space for larger items such as, water heaters, air conditioning units, and more. They are obviously popular with plumbers and HVAC people, but they are so useful for a wide variety of businesses, including remodelers.

Dump Bodies

This would include Flatbed Dump Bodies, Landscape Dump Bodies, Steel Dump Bodies, and Aluminum Dump Bodies.

A Flatbed Dump or Stakebed Dump is just a Flatbed or Stakebed with a hoist allowing one to dump a load. It can be used as any Flatbed or Stakebed most of the time and also perform dumping when that need exists.

A Steel Dump Body is committed to a certain variety of tasks, whereas the Flatbed Dump can perform many more. Steel and aluminum dumps are popular in snow areas for carrying salt and sand, using spreaders and snow plows, and more as well as popular in construction where heavy dirt, gravel, rock, and other loads need to be dumped. Having a Steel Dump Body with fold-down sides allows it to be loaded with a forklift to carry loads as a Flatbed might to extend the usefulness of this body.

The Landscape Dump is a Flatbed dump with some solid sides often made out of HD plywood or steel that may or may not be removable, along with a framed rear swing-away gate system. This body is designed for relatively light landscape trimmings, small branches, and other debris from landscape work, rather than dirt and other heavy materials.

Van Body

The Van Body is just a box on wheels. Those boxes come in different sizes and are made from different materials, such as aluminum sheet metal with steel cross members, or the much more durable FRP (Fiberglass Reinforced Plywood), which is how virtually all the rental vans are built. It is a drayage vehicle taking things from point A to point B. They can be mounted on Cutaway van chassis, tilt cab chassis, or standard chassis. They are very popular because they are great for keeping things hidden and out of the weather while delivering them from place to place.

Crane and Welder Bodies

These can be modifications of a Service Body or Flatbed type body. The main difference is they have a crane mounted somewhere on the body or they have welder compartments for carrying welder bottles and welding machines. There are about as many modifications of a

Crane or Welder Body as there are people who want one. These are also sometimes called Mechanic's Trucks.

Specialty Bodies

Everything else will be temporarily put into this category. This might include bodies that are specifically designed for a certain task or industry, such as a Glass Body, Street Sweeper, Beverage Body, and more.

Body Type Inventory Mix

To figure the best mix for a dealership, I would look at the report that was done at the beginning to see what is being used in your region. To help dealers in California stock a good mix of body types, I developed a formula that works extremely well. *Here it is:*

Contractor Bodies------------10%-15% of mix

USC Combo Bodies ----------5%-10% of mix

Flatbed and Stakebed ----------------20%-30%

Service or Utility Body --------------30%-45%

Plumber Style Body ------------------5%-10%

Van Body --------------------------15%-25%

Dump Bodies (All)--------------------5%-10%

Other Bodies------------------------5%-10%

This mix was designed to assist new dealers making the most of what they stock in terms of covering the market and turning inventory. The variance in the percentages of each body type is there to allow for regional differences. For example, in Northern California (Sacramento and North)

Service Bodies would probably be at the higher end of the percentage variance and in Central California (Stockton to Bakersfield), the Flatbed and Contractor Bodies would be at the higher end.

Generally this mix worked so well, we used it as a standard for every dealer I worked with in a wide geographic area. It would be as good a place to begin as I can imagine anywhere in the country.

Using this framework then makes it easy to see when the mix is out of line. When consulting with dealers, I used a form to check the stock at each dealership each week to see if the mix was in line.

At one dealership that I didn't work with, but checked their inventory in anticipation of doing business with them, I saw a very strange mix. They had 76 upfitted trucks and five empty chassis on the lot at the time I took the inventory. Since I still have the records from those sessions, here was their mix compared to our suggestions:

Contractor Bodies 10%-15% of mix ------ 49%
USC Combo Bodies 5%-10% of mix ------ 1%
Flatbed and Stakebed 20%-30% --------- 21%
Service or Utility Body 30%-45% ---------- 9%
Plumber Style Body 5%-10% ------------- 11%
Van Body 15%-25% ---------------------- 3%
Dump Bodies (All) 5%-10% -------------- 4%
Other Bodies 5%-10% -------------------- 3%

If you take the flatbed mix as a whole including Contractor, Flatbed and Dump Bodies, it equals 74%, the Service Bodies, USC, and Plumber as a group equals 21% and the Van Bodies, just 3%.

This mix is so skewed toward Flatbed products that you would think that was the only market they served. This is a very costly arrangement to carry that amount of stock in that one body type. In addition, almost all of the Contractor Bodies were heavy duty 450 and 550 units which are somewhat more costly than the 350 which normally does the job extremely well. Not only does this send the flooring line soaring, but misses so many opportunities for sales in other body types. If their dealer had this tool, they might like to rearrange this mix somewhat.

Again, as stated earlier, you would be stocking cargo vans and pickups with racks and so on if you're in the commercial market and those would be numbers on top of these. When I am referring to commercial upfitted inventory, I do not include those trucks. In addition to that, I do not count empty chassis in the mix either. This is strictly for stocking upfitted bodies.

The Mix within the Mix

The single most popular upfitted truck in California is a single rear wheel 8' Service Body, yet I wouldn't make my entire Service Body mix to be that one truck. The world wants variety and the commercial market does as well. If you did the analysis of the vehicles driving around or through your area, you will have noticed a lot of variety.

I might not even stock two of the same thing. So, for example in the Service Body area, I might stock one 8' Service Body with a rack on a SRW regular cab chassis, gas motor. Then maybe I'd stock an 8' Service Body with a rack on a SRW extended cab, diesel motor, then a 9' Service Body on a DRW with a rack and cargo bed enclosure, then an 11' Service Body on a DRW with a rack, master locking system, rack straps, vise bracket, and power inverter mounted in one of the cabinets. As you can see there are so many variables when you think about gas and diesel, 8' SRW, 9' DRW, 11' DRW that to carry two identical trucks will not allow a dealer to cover the market very well unless you carry a lot of trucks.

The idea I want to impart here is to mix it up and mix it up within the mix at the same time. Order some options and show off some features. Think about showing prospects things they may not have thought about, things they may not see on other dealer's lots, and so on. My experience has taught me that when I showed a prospect a better way or a better tool to help them make more money or work more efficiently…their loyalty stayed with me. To me, it's all about solutions for the end user and sometimes they just don't know about the wealth of optional features available that can save them time, money, and effort.

Partnering vs. Competing: Carry More Inventory Than You Have!

To maximize your inventory availability and allow you to essentially carry more inventory ready for immediate delivery than you actually have, it is essential in my opinion to partner with other dealers who stock your brand of upfitted trucks. It is a far superior arrangement than treating them as competitors.

Exchange inventory lists and help each other close more deals. Freely trade with other dealers, become familiar with what they stock, and seek ways to be of service to them and how they can be of help to you.

If you're going to be an aggressive dealer in commercial as I was, you are going to stock a number of units that no one else is willing to stock because of their conservatism. Having those other dealers' inventory available to you then allows you to be able to get the 'cookie cutter' units quickly when you need them. You don't have to stock multiples of them, thereby expanding your specialty inventory where much of the gross profit is.

Create a partnership network with a number of dealers. Help them and they will help you. There are so many ways this can be of mutual value. I know from my own experience that this is true when we approach other dealers as partners rather than competitors. There is plenty for everyone and it won't stop you or hold you back from creating a spectacular Commercial Truck Department. Rather, it will be of benefit.

Another effective way to have more inventory available than you have is to partner with your key body companies with bailment pool units. If you do a certain level of business with them, they may be willing to have some bodies prebuilt and mounted on chassis and have them ready to release to you immediately. You could have this in a couple of days rather than weeks. I know some who have made use of this and it helped them a great deal.

Aggressive Strategies on Inventory

This is a good place to inject one of my favorite and most successful strategies. Take full advantage, on purpose and as a strategy, when other dealers have something they are having a really tough time moving and they are ready to cut loose at a loss. These are grand opportunities.

Here are some examples of what I mean. I took a four-day road trip once to see every *Chevy, GMC,* and *Isuzu* commercial truck dealer I could in southern California. The purpose was to see how we were doing by comparing ourselves and our fledgling operation to some well-established and even some very large commercial truck dealerships. I was a *Chevy* dealer and brand new *Isuzu* Truck dealer. I found a brand new *Isuzu* NRR that was over two years old on this dealer's lot. He had a 14' Flatbed dump on it and I saw dollar signs. The bed was cheap and I thought that if I removed that bed and put a 14' Van Body on it, I could move it in a heartbeat. Then, I could put the Flatbed dump somewhere else.

After that much time, the dealer wanted it gone. I made him an offer at about $15,000 below invoice ($25,000 was the offer). He thought long and hard for many minutes and then said yes. I was thrilled. I had a Van Body installed on it, put the Flatbed dump on a different chassis that I thought was more suitable and saleable, sold the Van Body in two days, the dump bed in a couple of weeks, and made exceptional profits on both. I could have thrown the Flatbed dump away and still made a nice profit.

As another example, this is what I taught a dealer to do. *Ford* had the LCF tilt cab and it was a slow seller only because the dealers didn't know how to sell it. With my *Isuzu* Tilt-Cab experience, I taught this dealer how to sell the product. I also suggested he make some cash offers that would be a huge opportunity for a quick profit and at the same time a real benefit to help the other dealer turn stale inventory into cash. He bought several far below invoice, sold them at or near invoice, and made six to ten thousand a copy. There are some serious bargains all the time if you know what to look for, you are aggressive enough to seek them out, and are prepared to take advantage of them.

Here's another thing we did while consulting with a dealer. A customer wanted two 3/4-ton diesel pickups with 8' beds, of which there were none available in three states, along with a Flatbed truck. It just so happened that we had two Service Bodies in stock with the diesel engine. We dealer traded for two gas pickups, which were plentiful, and then swapped the beds to create the diesel pickups. That deal netted over $10,000 gross profit after all was said and done and we got it done in just a few days.

I was always on the hunt for those kinds of deals. Many of them I would find at bailment pool body companies. They might have a one or two-year-old unit and I would get a body for half price or less to take it away. In the meantime, I knew where I could move it, plus I was not afraid to stock it. I have a long list of these kinds of deals. It is sort of like being a 'picker' in one of those television shows.

I highly recommend this strategy for superior profits, and for just plain FUN! What a rush it is to make deals like that. These are almost always my highest profit deals.

Display and Inventory Visibility

Visible frontage is valuable real estate for any dealer. I recommend that a dealer give visible display to the Commercial Truck Department like this. Use your stocking percentage of overall inventory; e.g., 15% of inventory equals 15% of display space, so that people driving by see you are in the commercial truck market. Eventually, an aggressive dealer may even have a separate lot for their commercial operation. Many do that now and it can be very effective. In the meantime, sharing space with the retail side will work fine.

The focus on commercial trucks is the body. I would display units to show off the body, not the chassis. If you have a Dump Body, put the dump in the air and show it off as a Dump Body. I also recommend parking commercial units in odd positions not in a line like most retail dealerships do. Shake it up and do things a bit differently.

Although in a good commercial operation, most sales will be made by repeat and referral business and your ongoing prospecting, some sales will still be made by passersby that just happen to see something that catches their eye. So, I recommend putting the most interesting and attention getting units in that display area.

I used to share dealership frontage with retail and had only about 20% of the space, so I called it my 'Macy's Window Display'. I would order units specifically to put in that window space for the purpose of getting attention. For example, as a *Chevy* dealer, I ordered a 3500HD (no longer made but equivalent to a *Ford* F450 or *RAM* 4500), 84-inch CA chassis, 165-inch wheelbase in bright red and I mounted an 11' Service Body with shiny treadbrite lid covers and a black forklift loadable rack mounted on the inside edges of the Service Body compartments. Then I put on some 19.5' Alcoa Aluminum Wheels which were sent out and specially polished, put a good detail job on it and that truck just begged for attention. I put it on the point and someone driving by who lived 200 miles away came in and just had to have it. This happened over and over again with similar vehicles made to look like rock stars. Put a plain old white common body out there and it just disappears into the background.

Keep Them Clean and Ready To Drive

The retail units probably get washed once or twice a week depending on the season and the commercial units should be treated exactly the same. Cleanliness is just as important on them as the retail side—including the bed area!

They also need to be started regularly to make sure they are in running-ready condition. When someone comes in to look at a unit and you want to take them on a test drive, there is nothing worse than a dead battery. Unless, that is it is running on only a few of the available cylinders.

Make sure they are ready to deliver as much as possible. Vinyl sweat on the windows is a turn off, too. Invest in lot maintenance and it will pay off in sales.

If something needs attention, don't delay. Get the unit into the shop and get it handled now rather than later. If something on the body needs attention get it to the body company or have them come and take care of it.

Every unit on the lot should be ready to deliver any time.

Demonstrators

Most factories have a demo program with special incentives for putting a unit into demo service. In addition, through the bailment pool system, these demo programs are extended to the body companies and that allows extra demos to be secured at your dealership through that avenue as well. It is important and effective to make use of all of these programs to assist in showing these units to end users and helping to offset the costs involved.

Demos should be used in prospecting and in showing off units away from the dealership. Because of the miles put on the units, the offsetting demo allowances can help it to be a cost effective decision as well as a practical reason to have demos.

Managing Your Inventory

I've developed an Excel spreadsheet and I have used it for many years in my own operation and all of those where we have consulted. We offer it at no charge along with an explanation of how it works on one of our websites at www.commercialtrucksuccess.com.

This is a simple tool that is in two separate spreadsheets. One for stock units and the other becomes a database for sold and traded units. They are cut from the same cloth, so you can cut and paste from the stock spreadsheet into the sold one saving time and effort.

I said it is simple and it is. However, it is so valuable after a period of time only if it is kept up properly. It will provide a wealth of information to help you constantly improve your stocking choices, keep track of which units bring in more gross profits, and so on. Otherwise, it will be a guessing game.

Keeping up the spreadsheet is pretty easy if it is done a minimum of once a week and for an active organization, more often may make it more effective. It is as simple as adding new arrivals and moving sold units to the other file and then filling in a few blanks.

In addition to keeping track, this serves as a database to print inventory reports for sales teams and a number of other reports for management. I found this area to be one of the most important.

It keeps track of days in stock and days in flooring so you can see how you are turning your inventory, do something about marketing, and so on. It also has information in it about the cargo capacity of the unit, trailering capacity, chassis costs, body costs, MSRP calculations, and much more.

Of all of the tools I've developed to help my own operation and then to help others, I am sure that this one thing stands as the most helpful and valuable. In fact, this spreadsheet began as an MS-DOS database in 1989. It was a challenge, but I kept up the entries religiously in it of all the sales, gross profits, and much more. When I left that first operation after four years, I took a week off before beginning the second and in that time downloaded all the information in that database to create a blueprint of what we had achieved that amounted to a whole notebook full of charts, graphs, and numbers analyzed. That tool helped me get off to a tremendous start at the next operation and really showed me the value of keeping track. I recommend that you make use of it, or create your own with similar information and helps.

Bodies Are Not Necessarily Permanent

One of the interesting things about most upfitted commercial trucks is that the body can be transferred from one unit to another or taken off and put on the ground temporarily. It is not permanently mounted.

The body doesn't change value year to year like the truck does. But what does matter is the condition of the body. So, when a dealer has a one or two year old unit they want to move quickly, changing the body or removing the body may be a helpful option.

HOWEVER...

This is a two-edged sword. The fact that it can be removed is only one aspect of this. It also costs money to remove it or transfer it and if it is put on the ground, it can be damaged and it will continue to deteriorate in the weather. So, here are some guidelines you might find helpful to consider when it comes to removing or transferring bodies.

When you take a unit off and put it on the ground, make sure a new chassis is secured as quickly as possible to remount it on. In addition, charge all of the costs involved in removing and remounting in the future to the unit it was removed from. This keeps the body cost in line and doesn't create a false gross or false loss on the unit from where it came. Increasing the inventory cost in the future to help something now makes no sense.

If the body goes on the ground, always add some money for refurbishing unless it is going to be reinstalled very quickly because scratches will need to be touched up. Also, if a body goes on the ground, make sure the office knows about it and can account for it. Keep them abreast of any changes along with upper management. Keep it in the light.

Also, when swapping bodies from one truck to another to make a sale or otherwise move a unit, charge *all* of the swap costs against the unit being sold or traded. Again, there is no good to be had by increasing the inventory costs on stock units or recording false profits or losses.

Make sure all of your records and that of the office are updated to indicate very clearly what happened and how the inventory values have changed. In addition, if units are floored with the bank, they will need to be notified of the adjustment as well. A paper trail is critical. Also make sure that your own inventory and sold inventory spreadsheets reflect all of these changes with notes detailing what happened and why.

The ideal situation is that nothing is ever removed or swapped, but that is unrealistic in my thinking. I want to stress the importance of doing it professionally and with good accounting practices. The advantage is that it can be done when needed and it will absolutely be of benefit, it will help make more sales, turn old inventory without loss or with minimal losses, and more.

Turning Inventory

Of course, the ideal turn of inventory is to a customer paying you a profit and moving it prior to any flooring interest expense. Obviously, this will not always be the case. Here are some ideas to help turn inventory.

Make sure your dealer partners are aware of your inventory. Go so far as to point out some of those that you want assistance in moving.

Market them to your database via a monthly newsletter to bring attention to them. Market them also on your website, blog, social media, and so on to get maximum attention.

Consider swapping bodies. It is not ideal, but it can be a huge benefit sometimes. As an example, you might have an old unit that has an expensive body, say an 11' Service Body or something like that. You could swap that out with a plain Flatbed, allowing you to reduce the sales price by many thousands of dollars and perhaps even open a larger market audience as a result. This can be very helpful from time to time.

Again, I like to keep swapping to a minimum, but there are times when it is very helpful to take advantage of that option.

Dress it up. Another way I've moved a unit more quickly is to make it pretty. It is amazing what a set of Alcoa wheels will do for a commercial unit ... even a white one!

If it isn't too late, put it in demo service to get that additional incentive which can make the difference in moving it. You may have to put a minimum number of miles on it (usually around 500), but it may be worth it.

Sometimes you can get your body partner to help you incentivize the unit to move it. They want a new order and you may not be able to order it until you move the old one. This is a grand way to take advantage of your body partner and benefit them as well.

Put it on the point. Put it in the best display place you have. I'll never forget that whenever I had a demo I needed to move for whatever reason, I had it specially detailed and shined and put it on the showroom floor and it never failed to move it quickly. We don't have showrooms generally for the Commercial Truck Department, but using that same idea can be of assistance. Give it supreme attention.

Offer spiffs or other incentives to your crew. Many times when I had an old unit, I would offer a large minimum commission of at least $500 regardless of the accepted gross. Depending on the people you have this can be a huge help. I know I've had several salespeople that loved those deals and they sold them quickly.

Get the Whole Team Involved and Spread the Word

Create a flyer for this one unit or for just two units where you can give some detail about them and pass the flyer out in key locations.

I had one salesperson that sent out a minimum of 50 letters a day to his database and he always had a bargain section in the letter focusing on those kinds of units. It was a great help and we sold a lot of older units that way.

The main thing is to be aware how old units are and do exactly like grocery stores do in moving older items to the front in order to move them out. First in, first out, is always a great policy.

One of the problems created by rebates from the chassis manufacturers is that they eventually go away. As finance offers and rebate offers are changed, it becomes ever more important to pay attention to the age of inventory and turn it quickly. When it so happens that there are huge rebates that are about to disappear, it can be beneficial for the dealership to actually purchase the unit, take the rebate, and resell it as a used unit. It might be the best chance left to sell the unit with none or minimal losses. I have seen some dealerships take advantage of this and also many who fail to do so.

You will always have old units to deal with, whether it is on the retail side or the commercial side. Just make it part of your overall routine of marketing within and outside the dealership to do everything you can to move them in an effective way. Keep them moving and keep paying attention to the ones that need more attention. The inventory spreadsheet we told you about will help a great deal here.

Having old units is a given in my mind. It doesn't mean they were ordered wrong necessarily, although that could be the case. It is most likely a timing thing. After over 40 years in and around the auto business I know that every vehicle sells eventually and even those that some call sale-proof. Sometimes the ugly one wins the prize. I will never forget receiving a 1976 Chevy Nova at the end of the model run. Back then, the factory might substitute whatever they have left to get the unit out the door. This thing came in bright yellow with blue checkerboard seats and blue trim. It was so ugly I could hardly look at it, but the funny part is that it sold in less than two weeks. We even made a profit on the free flooring.

More Inventory Details

There is more about inventory such as making sure there is an addendum sticker on each truck describing the body, showing the additional cost and then a total MSRP, making sure inventory tags are not falling off, and on-and-on. This is pretty basic stuff. There are laws about various stickers as well. I think that each upfitted truck should have an addendum stating the upfit details and the price with a total MSRP so that the potential buyer has a good picture of the list price and then your sales price will make more sense. This helps when no one is on the lot to talk to as well.

Weight slips is a seriously important piece to have done ahead of time. In California, body companies routinely provide this certificate to dealers when they deliver the upfitted truck. Travelling to Washington state on a trip, I found that the body companies didn't do this service for dealers as they do in California, nor did the dealers do it for themselves. Consequently, these dealers didn't have weight slips so they had no good information about cargo capacity. In addition, it is normally required by DMV. Waiting until it is sold seriously compromises the delivery if you have to go get a weight slip or, heaven forbid, forget about it until after the delivery.

I suggest that you keep your inventory up to date including any addendums, stock numbers that can be seen, and so on. If you don't have a lot porter, then this should be done by the Commercial Truck Department as part of their duties.

SERVICE, PARTS, AND BODY SHOP

n my opinion, there is a huge opportunity for growth in the Service and Parts Departments in dealerships. Committing to the addition of an effective Commercial Truck Department provides even more opportunities.

Part of the reason I think it is such a huge opportunity is that in all the dealerships I have worked for, there are none that I would personally go to for service, though I tried them all several times. I've had negative experiences in every one of them. Keep in mind not every experience was negative. However, as a whole experience, I wouldn't return. From a loyalty point of view when I worked for that company, it only made sense I would take my vehicle to 'my' company's Service Department. I always gave them more opportunities as a result. But each dealership's Service Department seemed to have an attitude that was not helpful, like a doctor with a poor bedside manner. And in addition … they failed to do the work well or properly on several occasions.

In my travels, I have seen very similar things at far too many dealerships. I've talked with numerous commercial truck managers that cringe when someone needs to go to their Service Department. Immediately I can tell this dealership will never reach but a very small part of their potential as a result. Service is so important to the Commercial Truck Department's success. Instead, these commercial truck managers should be proud and thrilled to send their customers to their own Service Department.

In addition, as a sales manager in the business for 25 plus years, I saw service and sales at odds with one another frequently. It seemed ridiculous to me that this was even allowed to exist. Many dealerships have different standards for service than from the rest of the organization.

I won't go into any more detail about my experiences or my associates' experiences, but the main reason I bring it up at all is to show you how prejudiced I am in believing there is such an opportunity for more business in Service and Parts. Those departments could have had my business by treating me differently and by being good at what they do. I'm hoping your Service and Parts Departments are the exception. If they are, the commercial market will beat a path to your door once they know you are open to bringing service to that market.

So, let's talk about some of the opportunities in Service and Parts.

Increase the Level of Skill

Having been a journeyman level qualified auto mechanic prior to entering the auto business as a salesperson, I have a certain skill level and understanding of the machine, how to repair it well, and all of the potential problems possible in those very complicated machines. As a result of that experience, I absolutely appreciate it when I am in the presence of a truly good mechanic.

To me, the most needed thing on the planet relative to automobiles and trucks is to have people who can accurately and quickly diagnose a service-related problem. They are few and far between. My old (because he was even at that time) auto shop teacher used to refer to 'Joe McGee Mechanics' as undesirable ne'er-do-wells and he called most mechanics 'parts changers.'

If I were to run a Service Department, I would find a great diagnostician and he or she would never have to get their hands greasy again. I worked with one such artist in the Air Force.

All they would do all day long is diagnose problems. With one or two of these folks, all I would need would be parts changers to do the actual work. If I paid these people double what they were currently making, I would still make so much more profit with the efficiency of knowing what to fix and solving the problem the first time. In addition to that, word of mouth advertising would spread like wildfire throughout the area. When you take your vehicle to these folks, it is always fixed right the first time.

Seem like an ideal idea? The opportunity exists to improve dramatically and head toward that ideal. Along the way your profits will be ever-increasing and the business ever-expanding. Be the best that you can be and never stop improving.

The Commercial Market

Commercial trucks are used for work and businesses need them. Consequently when that truck is down, it is costing them money every minute that it is down. In addition, a downed vehicle creates a bottleneck of work. Problems mount as the vehicle is out of commission. So, it is of paramount importance that it be repaired as quickly and efficiently as is possible.

When it comes to maintenance of commercial vehicles, it is important to find ways to be of service to these businesses with as little interruption as possible. After all, they are being used for business

So many sales can be made over time by providing great service. A Service Department has the potential to increase not only their own business, but the sales department's business as well. It reminds me of that old phrase, 'the way to a man's heart is through his stomach.' Well, the way to a company's business is through great service.

Many companies may have a mix of light-duty and medium-duty trucks. It will be important to have service capacity and capability for both to ensure that you can capture and take care of as much of a company's service as possible. For the purpose of this book, we are focused on light and medium-duty trucks, while leaving heavy-duty trucks (class

8 and above) off the menu. That is a very different commercial truck market.

You must have equipment that can lift vehicles in the air with bodies on them and have lifts that can handle the weight of loaded medium-duty trucks. In addition you need specific tools, so there is an investment required to deal with this market. However, the returns down the road will make that investment look very small.

Just as in sales, one of the best things about aggressively going after the commercial truck market is all the other business that is secured as a result.

Priority Service

Due to the nature of how the vehicles are used and how important they are to the company that uses them, offering priority service is a key ingredient to success in serving the commercial market.

Those dealerships that have signed up for factory commercial programs like *RAM's* Business*Link, Ford's Business Preferred Network, Chevy's Business Central or Business Elite,* and so on are supposed to have a separate service writer for commercial customers as well as priority service for those clients. In addition, they are encouraged to have extended hours to help accommodate the commercial customer. Anything you can do to cater to the commercial customer will be beneficial.

Some dealerships have service until midnight or they have mobile service to do routine maintenance onsite for their commercial clients. Many also offer a pick-up and delivery service. The clients don't mind paying for service like this. It is beneficial in many ways for them, so they will be very pleased to have you offer more convenient and more effective service.

Get them in and out with speed and efficiency and make it a pleasant experience.

Frankly, I think every customer, retail, and commercial should get the same priority service. Treating every customer in this manner will do wonders for your service business.

Attracting the Commercial Business

The Commercial Truck Sales Department has a prospecting program of going out and visiting businesses to make themselves known. This is an excellent opportunity to offer service. Giving the sales team a flyer or other handouts is good. You could also hire a team member to prospect along with the sales team, so there is someone more specifically knowledgeable about service. Then go in focusing on service and not sales.

I am confident that in prospecting, going after the service business will be the first priority and the best hope of getting any of the potential client's business. People and companies don't need vehicles very often in comparison with the need for service and maintenance. That is a perfect place to start.

This also speaks to how closely Service and Parts Departments need to work with the Commercial Sales

Department for the overall success of the operation. They need each other and the better that relationship and the more closely they are in their thinking, the more their potential success.

I think that the Service Department would be best served to team up with the Sales Department and do marketing together. One of the best marketing tools is a newsletter, so gathering email information for your database is important. It would be very cost effective to share all of the Internet marketing with the Service and Commercial Sales Departments. Again, the more they work together, the more success each will have.

In fact, I think that an excellent Service Department wanting to grow their commercial business is the biggest benefit to the Commercial Truck Sales Department. I can hardly stress this enough. It is a key ingredient to the long-term success of the whole program.

I've seen a couple of Service Departments who really went after the commercial market in a big way. They expanded their facilities and within a relatively short period of time, their commercial business was their greatest asset and profit center. I've also seen one where their Sales Department was weak in comparison, yet the dealership benefitted across the board as a result of the Service Department's aggressive strategy.

In any case, the best strategy for attracting new business is taking excellent care of the business you already have.

— CHAPTER FOUR —

MARKETING STRATEGIES

Overview

The overall marketing strategy of the Commercial Truck Department should be prospecting and relationship building. This is different from most retail departments who typically use advertising as traffic building. It has long been my experience and that of most others in commercial trucks that this particular market has a very high rate of repeat and referral sales. That comes from relationship building. Prospecting and networking will be our main method of advertising.

We use a multi-faceted approach to attract sales that includes database marketing, regular mailers (can be email) such as newsletters, specific mailers (can be email) such as special offers, traditional advertising with focus on commercial, commercial style publications, Service and Parts Departments, telephone (for appointment or info gathering), networking, in-person prospecting, merchandising lot or displays, offsite displays, referrals, and Internet marketing.

Database Marketing

I would begin with the single most important thing that helped me get the success I was able to achieve. Buying a database of businesses in and around the city the dealership is in is in is an important step. In my first operation, I was in a city of approximately 100,000 people at the time. We bought the list for that city as the first purchase and then added the whole county. We went on to add the five counties that surrounded that county and this 10,000 name list was our gold mine. In fact, it proved to be solid gold.

Buy the best list that you can get. Many companies with database lists now rent them. You pay an annual fee and can download a certain number per year which is included in that fee. This will be fine. We want to know who the businesses are and we will begin our marketing to this group, utilizing a combination of in-person visits, telephone contacts, and direct mail. As we make those contacts, we will continually update the database refining it and enhancing it.

Networking

Another way to get off to a good start is networking in your city. Get involved with the Chamber of Commerce in your city and surrounding cities. If your dealership is not already a member, now may be a good time. Most Chamber of Commerce organizations have mixers and other events like ribbon cuttings, grand openings, etc. where people can gather to network with each other. You can often get a list of all the business members and begin a soft marketing awareness campaign with that group. If your city is connected to another or is within less than 10 miles, it may be a good idea to become members of more than one Chamber.

Another effective way of networking is by joining a networking club. Many of these require paid dues. Some that require dues are LeTip or BNI and both of these can be very effective at getting business. I know that in our company, LeTip has made a dramatic difference in our business.

In many cities, there are other networking organizations who do not charge dues and you should consider joining. Many of these can be an effective way to spend lunchtime or breakfast time.

Some of this networking will require some after hour's participation for evening events. Those can be the most fruitful and I'm sure that scheduling can be worked out to everyone's benefit.

It is important at networking events that we keep the selling very low-key and have a very good 20-30 second statement of what we do, how we do it, and what is unique about us.

Once again, involving the Service and Parts Department by passing out their flyers of service and parts specials at these events can help generate traffic and potential relationships for future business.

Prospecting In-Person Advantages

Overall, in-person prospecting will be the most effective method of marketing for the Commercial Truck Department.

It is very important that a system be used in doing this so that it gets done and, more importantly, that it gets done regularly.

It is very easy to go out a few times, then get busy with quotes and other things, and put off prospecting that day to take care of the 'busy-ness'. But it only takes a day or two of missed efforts at prospecting and it can easily become a habit to avoid it. It needs to be every day—especially in the early stages of the Commercial Truck Department. We offer management tools that can be very helpful in this process.

There are two main advantages to in-person prospecting. One is they get to see you and the other is that you get to see them. Seems obvious, but those are the advantages. You can't see them on the phone or in the mail, nor can they see you. You have no idea what their business looks like and they most likely have never been to yours. However, let's go deeper about this.

The advantage of seeing them is not only meeting them and actually seeing people, but seeing their operation, what it looks like, the condition of repair, the kind of equipment they use, the kind of vehicles they use, the number of employees and what they do for the company, whether they have multiple locations or offsite warehouses, and such. You can see what kind of office equipment many of them have and how new or old it might be. You can see the repair of the building and their housekeeping habits, how they display merchandise if they sell merchandise, and how fresh or old much of that merchandise is.

You can get an idea of their marketing just by virtue of seeing their operation. Obviously, we want to see what kind of trucks or vans they use, how they are configured, how they might use them in their work, and so on. You will also get a really good feel about how they treat you when you go into their business. In fact, there is so much that you can learn in just a few minutes about the business that you could write many pages about what you see in that short time—if you're paying attention.

Prospecting Strategy

Our strategy is to learn anything and everything about that business in the few minutes that may be available. Telling them about us is secondary to this.

Here's the first overall strategy about prospecting that must be understood. You are not here to sell anything. You are here to observe, collect data, get to know a little about them and what they do, briefly introduce yourself, and leave a few giveaway items such as ink pens, notepads, or other logo marked small giveaways. There is nothing to reject other than your friendliness. That takes the heat out of making the call in the first place. In fact, it would be arrogant to think you could walk in and make a sale without first building some kind of relationship.

After we get information, see the operation, introduce ourselves, leave a few small trinkets as a gift, and understand their use of vehicles, we need to see if there is anything we can offer that will help them, 1) Make more money, 2)

Save money, or 3) Do their job more effectively or efficiently. Then a secondary appointment is to be made as soon as possible, if they are willing. So again, most of what we do on the in-person prospecting visit is observe and gather data.

The best we could hope for in my opinion is to meet the owner or main manager, see and understand how they use their vehicles in their business, see a need that we think we can satisfy, make a follow up appointment, and be on our way. It will be at that second appointment that any selling takes place ... other than selling yourself, of course.

Even if we don't get to meet the owner or main manager, there is much to learn that can lead us to a possible second appointment and potential for earning their service business and/or sales.

As we gather the data on each prospect call, a form is filled out in detail to record as much as possible about that contact for our master database. It is very important to build a database of information that will benefit the dealership after we have gone. If a follow up appointment is desired, decide on an approximate date for follow up.

It is all very non-threatening and easy. The prospect gets some gifts and you get to see their operation. The first contact should always be this easy.

So, here is the prospecting plan in an outline form that we have used in consulting with dealers:

Prospecting Plan

Gather information/observe everything

- Pay attention to every detail. Observe building and repair of building, employees and equipment, vehicles used in business, employee's vehicles, size of operation, etc.

- Give gifts and introduce ourselves

  ○ Service coupon, parts coupon, employee purchase program, notepads, etc. (Gifts are a key ingredient). Drives business to service in short period.

  ○ Along with packet of information, specials, etc.

  ○ Determine who buyer is and gather contact information.

Determine needs

This is where commercial truck training comes to play. We must determine if we have a product or service that will:

- Make them money

- Save them money

- Help them do their job better/more efficiently

If we have something that will do one or more of these things, we will put together a presentation and *make an appointment.*

Follow-up decision

- Will they be followed or deleted from the database

- If followed, when and how?

- All information given to commercial activities administrator

We have used this plan very effectively since 2006. It is an excellent way to do in person prospecting and achieve good results.

Offsite displays

One very good way of getting exposure to your inventory and do effective prospecting is to have offsite displays. These can be done at places like The Home Depot®, Lowe's®, lumber yards, and such. Sometimes you can participate with one of those vendors on a customer appreciation day or some other like event they may have. Sometimes you can team up with contractor group organizations, county fairs, and virtually any event that will draw people that may have potential prospects for what you sell.

Regarding the chain stores, the manager at each store will generally be the decision maker even though they may say corporate does that. We've seen a lot of variance in who will and who won't be helpful. One key ingredient to help make it happen and also make it effective for you is to act like a partner and offer to help them promote something that they want to promote.

At the chain stores and lumber stores, etc., it is a good plan to come very early, just before they open. Then stay only until around 10 a.m. unless they have a longer event where you are participating. This way, they can see you are not going to be messing with their parking area during their bigger traffic times and it sometimes makes it more palatable to allow you to have your display.

We also advise that it is necessary and highly beneficial to buy giveaways and have drawings. Buy all the giveaways at that store. Be a good partner and patronize their store. It also doesn't hurt to let the store manager know that you will be buying several giveaway items from them each time!

The raffle is the best way to gather contact information. Make the prizes worth entering. I suggest a budget of $100 to $300 per display event so you can buy some worthy prizes. Have a form that is really easy to fill in and accept business cards in lieu of the form. Make it easy to enter. One sale can make up for the expense of several display events, but a better way to look at it is advertising. In that regard, this is an extremely minor investment.

I also recommend that you offer free coffee and maybe some snacks. If there is a coffee vendor on the premises I recommend you partner with them for the coffee. At The Home Depot and some Lowe's that we have worked with, they had a food and drink vendor on premises. We made an agreement with them to accept a ticket from any customer and we would pay them at the end of our event for each coffee. Partnering always yields benefits.

Have an attractive unit to display and change it up each time. I recommend you try to do these events as often as possible. An ideal situation would be twice a week for offsite events. Although, do not have both in the same week at the same place. We've set up deals with certain Home Depot stores where we could go there once a week from opening until 10 a.m. and that benefitted everyone. We purchased the prizes from The Home Depot, the customers got a chance to win, and we gained a list of people to follow up with and to make potential sales.

In California, for instance, you have to have a special permit to sell at an offsite location. These are hard to get, so to be legal, we put a big sign on the vehicle that it is not for sale at this location and we never talk about prices. However, we can talk about the product all we want and still show it off and that works just fine.

In our prospecting plan of action for the commercial sales person, an offsite display event counts as a day of prospecting.

The offsite display can be an effective and profitable venture. It is a great way to show off unique items and try to bring attention to your offerings in a non-threatening way. The key with these is to do them as often as you can and to be professional by having literature with business cards, raffle tickets, sign-up forms, maybe a pop-up tent, and such and to have fun. This is not hard work. Make it fun and have a good time and the people passing by will too.

The offsite display is a perfect place to promote the Service and Parts Department specials with handouts, small gifts *(logo branded is preferred)*, and other promotional materials.

Advertising

Some of the places where advertising dollars can be effective are Trader publications and other truck marketing publications. For almost eight years, I had a full page double truck ad in the "Big Truck and Equipment Trader Magazine". Over time it consistently generated a profit and aided sales, especially in out-of-market areas, so that the vast majority of those sales were incremental sales. I found that the key to those publications was promoting 'used' and 'unique' vehicles. Standard things were advertised by a lot of people trying to compete over the lowest gross profit trophy, but I preferred making decent profits selling anything used and new items that were different or hard to find.

Other advertising that can be effective might be contractor associations and other associations where potential buyers may see your ad.

As a general rule, in a new commercial truck operation, traditional advertising is the last thing on the list if there is still money to spend. If the market is strong, it is less of an issue than when the market is weak.

Telephone

I hate cold calls and I hate getting them, too, so I do not promote cold calls. To me, the telephone is only good for making an appointment or gathering information. Some people are good at making cold calls effective, but they are very rare. If you find one, let them lead.

Referrals

Referrals are the best business you can get other than repeat sales. They are the easiest to close and the closing ratio is very high, so anything we can do to enhance referrals is good.

The best thing you can do is be very good at what you do and have a great team including Service and Parts. This will do more for encouraging referrals than anything I know.

I do recommend asking for referrals. If you have a happy customer, they should be very open to referring others to you and maybe even giving you an introduction here and there.

Generally, referrals take a little time. Within a year of beginning a commercial operation, you should be getting a small percentage of referrals and growing every year.

Mailers (or E-mailers)

Regular Mailers

Regular scheduled mailers such as newsletters are excellent and the key to these is consistency and interesting content. We recommend email newsletters because they are more interesting and effective in comparison with regular mail, as well as so inexpensive in comparison. I recommend when you do this and you do it every month and once a month is good.

Specific Mailers

This would be a special offer, a flyer with special information, and so on that is sent out when needed to a specific list. The advantage of database marketing is that you can target certain types of clients that have a much higher likelihood of responding to your specific offer. For example, you may have a Contractor Body that needs to find a home and you would then create a great flyer, download the list for that target market, and send them out.

This can also be email if you have an email list. Chances are, the email list will be developed as part of your prospecting and will take time to develop. Initially direct mail will be an effective way to get this out, along with your Internet marketing.

Internet Marketing

I believe very strongly in the power of Internet marketing. This is the main reason that I own an Internet marketing business called Upward Trend. Internet marketing is a very effective way to build your business over time. This is not a quick fix, but a building process. Get started and keep building month in and month out and it will pay off handsomely.

There are many tools in Internet marketing. One is a website. We think of this as a filing cabinet where everything that people might want to know about you and what you do and how you do it is there. If people ask questions, the answers should be on that site.

Another extremely effective tool is a blog. This works in combination with a website in many ways, as it is more current information generally presented in a linear format. The good news is that each post has its own URL, or web address, so the more posts you make over time, the more effective the blog can be at directing traffic to your operation. The blog should be constantly growing. It is the layering of posts that is most beneficial.

Then there is social media. It is all the rage at the moment and constantly changing. We use *Facebook, Twitter, LinkedIn, YouTube, Pinterest,* Networked Blogs, and more. These tools can really make a difference over time as well. It is instant communication with those that have become friends.

Email HTML newsletter. This is one of the most powerful tools for a commercial truck operation. Generally it is best used to market to your existing clients or friends. A lot of businesses forget about actually marketing on purpose to their existing clients. This is where the newsletter shines. We recommend once a month as a minimum. Since it should be rare to do more than this, it should be fairly easy to do. Doing this regularly and consistently is the key to its success. You want people to expect it and appreciate it.

Doing all of these in unison is extremely powerful, and this is exactly what we do to help dealers and other businesses. At Upward Trend, we offer what is called the Trend Setter Package (www.trendsetterpackage.com). Everything we do, people and businesses can do for themselves. However ... what we offer is doing it for them. That is the key ingredient because most people and businesses haven't the time to deal with it, keep it full of content, and consistently expand it. Still, if you have the time to do it yourself or in house, this process is very effective and will continually be more effective as time passes, IF it is consistently expanded. If you don't have time, we offer that service, or you might hire someone else to do it for you.

Keyword Buying and Internet Advertising is another area that can be done. This is common on the retail side of the dealership. You create a budget, buy some keywords, and then when people click on it, the vendor deducts an amount from your account. This is how many businesses get noticed in the search engines. The best way is using content, not keywords. Buying keywords can be effective particularly in the near term. You can also advertise on the Internet on various websites, blogs, newsletters, search engines, and so on.

Additional Information on Websites, Blogs, Social Media, and More

Website

We recommend a separate website for the commercial truck operation, with a link to the commercial site from the retail site and back from the commercial site to the retail site.

Why a separate website? Because a typical dealership website is lacking in content and is more focused on what I call 'factory marketing.' In the commercial department, we have a lot to talk about and share and this content is all searchable. It will benefit us in search engine searches as well as in content that people see when they come to the site. For example, you can have weight information, special commercial driver's license information, and so on at your site. Anything that people need to know about commercial trucks in general can be of help.

In addition, you can show off products in a more effective way and do a lot of things with content, photos, video, and more that will greatly benefit your sales and your clients.

Another reason is additional search recognition. The more signs that are out there ... the more opportunity to be found.

This site should be updated regularly and continually expanding, unlike most sites that are built and then very little gets changed after that.

Blog

Why a blog? A blog is basically just a website that is linear; sort of like a diary in that each post has a date with the newest post is on top. Blogs let your reader know what is happening now as well as the latest thing out there. Blogs also have sidebars for your readers to be able to see information and links about your operation and dealership.

Since everything that is on there is searchable via the Internet, the blog can be a huge help to get readers and traffic driven to your dealership sites and physical location. In addition, each and every post has a separate URL, so it shows up as a specific page. As time passes, the numbers of posts increases and so it is being more and more helpful in helping people find you.

On the side bar or sidebars, you have information about you, your team, the website, and all sorts of valuable information.

We want the content to be very interesting so that people want to come back to it again and again. This means all kinds of related content. Use videos, etc. and keep your own selling messages moderate. There are many *YouTube* videos produced by the main auto manufacturers, as well as other sources, that have fun, informative, and interesting content.

Social Media

This is a hot topic as of this writing and getting hotter by the moment. I dare say that it has taken the world by storm. *Facebook* is the number one social site at the moment and

I recommend you make good use of *Facebook* by using both a personal page and a business page. In addition, *Twitter* is a very good site to make use of and you can have a business page and a personal page there if you want. You will need two email addresses to do so. *LinkedIn* is what I call the *Facebook* for business people. It is great because it comes up in searches very nicely and it is also a great place to network.

Other social sites that are currently popular and can be helpful are *Pinterest*, *Tumblr* (a blogging program), and *Google+*. The list is very long and constantly changing. It is not an option to not do this, especially in *Facebook*, *Twitter*, and *LinkedIn*. So plan on doing it or finding someone to do it for you ... but do it. It is so powerful. It cannot be ignored any longer.

YouTube is one of the hottest social media sites now and it is also hot as a search engine. Make videos and get them on *YouTube*, then to your blog, then to social media, and more. *YouTube* is a must.

Here is a good place to add a comment about what I've seen typically at dealerships on this issue. Almost all of those I've seen (and there are many!), have their Internet so "locked-down" to prevent their employees from searching certain sites and much more. Out of fear, most will not even allow employees to view a *YouTube* video, to go to *Blogger.com* blogs, and much more.

If you think about how powerful the Internet social media can be (and it is!), then think about the benefit to the dealership of having all your employees tweeting on *Twitter* and commenting on *Facebook* and *Google+*. The information they put out there is invaluable about the specials you have going on, how fun it is to work here, what a wonderful person the dealer is, the newest product arrival, and much, much more.

This reminds me about the story of taking the lemon and making lemonade. This could be such a benefit. But, the "controllers" within the dealership want to shut it all down, as if that would work anyway. Everyone has a cell phone, so you cannot totally stop it—only on your computers. It would be so much better to unlock it and encourage people to be your social media team. You will own the Internet!

Email Newsletters, Event Marketing, and Surveys

This is probably the single most powerful tool in your Internet marketing arsenal. Start gathering email addresses of people who would like to receive a monthly newsletter from you and get going. Start with what you have and build from there.

Keep the selling to a minimum in the newsletter and make it as interesting as you can so that people will enjoy receiving it and want to keep receiving it. If you are doing nothing but promoting your products and your dealership, that will get old in a hurry. We recommend four keys to a good newsletter: Inform, Promote, Provide Value, and Entertain. It should be educational so that people learn something interesting, provide value in having links to things that can benefit them, or other ways you can add value to their lives. It should have something fun or funny such as a funny *YouTube* video or something else. Lastly, you should do some promoting of you and your company ... but that will take a back seat to the rest.

The back seat is the key to the whole Internet idea. You want to attract people and provide value for them so that they enjoy the experience, and in the process they find out things about you and what you do.

The Next Big Thing ...

The Internet is young and evolving very rapidly and there will always be new things coming down the pike. So, it is both wise and empowering to be as aware as you can about the various tools that are available and what is getting hot and what is not any more. Some of them come and then they are gone. It is to be expected in this extremely fast-paced social media atmosphere. Just stay abreast of what is going on as much as you can. You may find subscribing to some Internet publications helpful. Type "Internet publications," or "Internet magazine," into your search engine and you will find a great deal of information available to choose from.

Summary

By using all of these methods of marketing, you will have a prosperous department and find that this marketing strategy to be extremely effective and constantly growing in effectiveness moving forward.

— CHAPTER FIVE —

PERSONNEL

The Commercial Truck Department Needs a Team

At Commercial Truck Success, we promote the team concept for a Commercial Truck Department. Putting one person in there and hoping they do some justice in this very lucrative market is a dream. I know many dealers try to run with only one person. But, no matter how good a person you find, you still only have one person.

One person creates a number of problems. First … is the obvious fact you are putting everything into one person. Then, something changes. They may move away, quit, or get fired and everything that was built is now coming apart very quickly. You try to stick someone else in there to save it and it never does get saved. Over the years I've seen this so many times and every time it happens, it is sad. Some dealers never recover and they end up closing their commercial department, others give up the dream and accept mediocre results, and a few reformulate and find a better way.

Even if everything worked very well with that one person, they can only be expected to produce a certain result.

The opportunity in the Commercial Truck Department is far greater than one person can satisfy. In addition, since outside prospecting is such a benefit, this job rarely if ever gets done with a one person operation. They are always at home base.

Even starting small, there needs to be a team in order to be more effective. Yes, it will cost more up front. But, the return will be far greater. I typically recommend a minimum of a department manager, outside salesperson, and an administrative assistant. As the operation grows, additional salespeople will be added. You are starting with a wonderful foundation for which to grow quickly and effectively.

The commercial truck manager will be the leader and teacher of the operation. This person should come from within the ranks of managers rather than from the sales staff. Good salespeople do not make good managers as a general rule in my experience. Each has a different part and allowing them to play that part works out best.

Skills to look for in the manager include an understanding of sales, organization, leadership, teacher, and encourager. This person will direct the sales staff, train and teach the sales staff, and uplift and encourage the sales staff as well as be a servant to that staff. We need a good manager. If they have a passion for trucks, that would be a great combination.

Sometimes dealers will want a selling manager. This is back to the one person idea, trying to find one person who can do it all well. A good basketball or football team does not have the coach out on the floor taking shots or making passes. Nor do the star team players stand on the sidelines, to coach and lead the team. They are two different jobs that require two different sets of skills. It is no different here.

One thing I have learned about good salespeople in my over 40 years as a sales manager...the best utilization of a salesperson is to have them in front of prospects and customers building relationships making and reinforcing sales. It is also my experience that these salespeople are not very good at paperwork, detail, and organization. What they are good at is talking to and influencing people. That is where I want to have them the majority of the time.

In many dealerships, a salesperson may only spend a very small amount of time actually talking to prospects or customers and the rest of the time, they try to get them to do other things. I don't think this is effective for them or the dealership. In the Commercial Truck Department, we want to release the salespeople to do more selling and unburden them with so much of the rest. The salesperson will be focused on talking to people about products and services every day. They will function as an outside salesperson going into businesses and prospecting customers for potential sales. This salesperson will spend a great deal more time actually talking to prospects and clients.

In order to have that happen consistently and effectively, we need to manage it for them as much as possible. This is the main reason to have a manager and an administrative assistant. We keep the paperwork to a minimum for the salespeople. They can then move and talk to people while the other team members do what they do best in handling details and organizing activities.

The Team and Their Functions

The activities of the commercial truck manager will be primarily focused on growing this department as a business within a business. He or she will coordinate sales strategies with the Service and Parts Departments and build strong relationships with them. The manager will organize the time of the sales staff members with the help of the administrative assistant, organize training of the sales staff and other members, seek outside training, and teach the sales staff. This includes going on sales calls with the salespeople to ensure the training is effective.

The manager will order and manage the inventory while the administrative assistant helps keep track of and creates reports for management. They will also manage a myriad of details of information coming into and going out of the department.

Their main focus is growing the business. Helping create opportunities and managing time and activities to be the most effective is an important part of their duties. Delegating some activities may be necessary to keep workloads within reason.

The salesperson's activities will be focused on creating and expanding sales opportunities. Much of that will be done via prospecting. This means that this person is outside of the office a minimum of two to three hours each day, doing off-site events, talking to prospects and customers, expanding influence, loyalty, and good will. This needs to be done in a systematic way. It will be managed by the commercial truck manager and the administrative assistant to keep the salesperson on track and consistent.

For prospecting to be effective, it needs to be consistent. It is a common pattern for a salesperson to go prospect for a few days, then get busy doing quotes and use that as an excuse to stay at their desk. Prospecting then goes by the wayside. We cannot allow that to happen. We must manage the activities.

We can't really manage the results but we can influence the results. This is achieved by managing the activities, doing the training, following up, and overseeing all of it. I remember hearing my favorite mentor, Jim Rohn say, "the purpose of training is to find out who you have." I have found that to be very true. By managing these activities effectively, we will find out soon enough whom we have.

We may need to make adjustments along the way with a salesperson, up to and including changing them out for someone else. The key is that they do the activities as prescribed by the commercial truck manager and if the manager is doing their full job, they will see if the salesperson is being productive or not. There will be appointments if they are productive and those will lead to sales.

When you have a salesperson that is not productive, you may need to make the change and get on to a better candidate. By productive, I don't mean sales in the short term, because they take a while to materialize; however, appointments and other activities are a must and should happen regularly. I know in some cases I liked the person very much, but held on to them too long. They were just being unproductive. It's not helping anyone by continuing when someone is not going to work out. Training is a perfect way to find out.

At Commercial Truck Success, we have a system for prospecting and the organization of it. This system tracks the results, is simple to manage, and utilizes the team approach. I cannot express enough how important it is for everyone concerned to have a good system and be able to see results over time in a way that helps make the best decisions. It serves the bottom line as well.

The Administrative Assistant is a key person to the team. This person is going to act as a helper from time to time by answering the phone, taking a unit to service, or whatever may be needed to help a sale along. But their main duties will be to help the commercial truck manager manage the activities of the department in a very efficient manner. By taking the burden off of the sales focused team members (and it is a burden to salespeople and managers), this person can help the sales process get done much more effectively. The administrative assistant helps keep the unnecessary detail work away from the manager and sales staff and lets them focus on what they do best. Administration work is not what good managers or sales people do well. In my experience, this works out to be a perfect combination of team members.

What makes a great team at a Commercial Truck Department? In a word … passion. They love what they do and they are doing what they love. In another word … career—long term. It's not just about the money, although we all know that money is important. It's about them enjoying what they are doing. In another word … fun. They have fun doing it. Why? Because it is interesting for them and they get to help people solve transportation issues or help improve their business. It can be very satisfying. This team will love working with each other as well to make the team much more effective.

The Perfect Commercial Sales Representative

In my experience, it is someone who's been involved in the trades. In other words, they understand how these vehicles are used and they can understand the end user point of view. If they had zero knowledge about commercial truck specs, they would certainly understand the basic need and uses of a commercial truck. The specs are easy to teach, the other is not so easy.

This person is pleasant to talk to and makes friends easily. Someone who is outgoing enough to begin a conversation with a stranger and find common ground quickly is important. They tell good stories and talk with enthusiasm.

This person understands our business model without having to know all the ins and outs of it. I don't have to teach them a whole lot of philosophy, but instead the steps and the basic procedures. Philosophy takes time to teach, procedures is easy.

This person is not happy sitting at a desk, but likes being out and about talking with clients, meeting new prospects, helping do what needs to get done. They are used to doing and like to be busy. They hate being bored.

The ideal person would also be excited about not having a cap on earnings and is not interested in how much an hour. Instead, they want more control over their earnings and want to experience some of their potential by exercising their own initiative rather than waiting for a raise.

So, when we find this person, we must close the deal. Until that person comes along, we do the best we can.

Where to Find Good People?

I know where it is not … in the newspaper. I gave up using that medium a very long time ago. The people it brings in are not what we are looking for. Well, to be fair, I think the odds are about 95 to 1. It is possible, but you will have to do a lot of wading.

Probably the best source is referrals. This is really good because you can get a good idea who they are through the referral source even if they embellish, which is a given. This is also good because it is a way people can connect before they leave their existing employer. They may have expressed their feelings about where they now work and have now opened the door to communication.

Like people attract like people, so the person refer-ring someone to you will probably have numerous charac-teristics of the person they refer. This also helps in making higher quality contacts to choose from.

Another good place to look for salespeople is in the retail market. Many times retail businesses, such as you find in the mall, pay poor wages, slightly above minimum wage. Even retail store managers make small salaries in comparison with what can be made outside of retail. Here's an opportu-nity for somebody who wants to make sales a career, who would like to do better and who would be willing to make the investment in learning how to do something different and better. They still have to be somebody who is going to be able to go out and do the tasks.

If you are active in *LinkedIn*, this can be a good place to recruit people. *Craig's List* is another good source to see information on people seeking positions. Then there are the paid sites such as Monster.com and others.

Another good way is by networking. Letting people we meet in networking situations know of an opportunity for employment can be helpful. Networking events, such as Chamber of Commerce mixers, networking clubs, social clubs, service clubs, and other organizational opportunities are good places for sharing employment opportunities.

One of the worst places in my long experience is hir-ing from other dealers. I like the concept of finding a really good salesperson with a great following who is unhappy at the store he or she is at, can bring the majority of those clients with them, and be an instant and profitable success in this operation. I've just never seen it work that way exactly.

First ... why are they unhappy and what does that mean? How will the new place create happiness? Really good salespeople don't like to change places because they know full well how hard it is to take their clients elsewhere. In addition, a dealer who knows they have a great salesperson and is a smart businessperson would be taking care of any unhappy situation with that person. So taking people from another dealer is not what it is made out to be. However, it can also be an opportunity under the right circumstances. I have seen it work out once in a while, yet I am just very suspicious about it and would check it out thoroughly.

Finding good people is an art and I am always looking for good people, even today, whether I need them now or not. I have found that strategy to be very useful.

Pay Plans

After over 25 years in the auto business in many capacities and in my association with dealers since then, I've seen and also experienced a lot of different pay plans. At most, dealerships commission only is the desired pay plan. In commercial, I've come up with something better. Essentially, it is a salary plus commission plan.

There are many reasons for this. The number one reason is that it is a prospecting organization and this allows us to insist it be done. A dealer could look at this salary as an advertising expense if they like, and essentially that is what is being done in the prospecting.

Another reason is that it provides a certain confidence or feeling about the company they are working for, who is taking care to ensure they make a decent living. Sure we need sales made. That is a given, but more important to that cause is the consistent building of good relationships with potential buyers through prospecting and getting people into service and so on. The salary goes a long way to help ensure these things are done effectively.

The salary at this writing would range from $1500 to $2500 per month depending on the candidate and skill levels. The commission percentage would be less than is typical in a commission only program, yet there will be plenty of motivation to go far beyond these modest salary levels.

The best pay plans that I have used consist of the salary plus commission spread based on number of sales, growing in percentage and retroactive to number one, along with a gross profit bonus at accumulated monthly gross levels with growing bonus as the gross hits certain levels. This three-fold multi-level approach has been most effective for me in encouraging and rewarding performance. One of the best parts of it is the gross bonus because we want our staff to not forsake gross profits just because they have the authority to make a lesser deal. This way they are rewarded for their attention to the needs of the dealership and its success.

TRAINING

Overview

There is a definite advantage to knowing with confidence. This is where training can be a useful tool.

It has been my experience that people can easily learn in order to repeat certain things, remember dates, some features, benefits, etc., but that doesn't mean they understand it. It is understanding that makes a huge difference in an effective commercial truck operation and training is a key ingredient toward that result.

There is always something more to learn, so there will always be a need for training. However, it need not be overwhelming or on a schedule that turns people away. It needs to be interesting, fun, and useful. It needs to be relevant and current. It should be timely and worthy of everyone's time including student and teacher.

I'll never forget learning about a rag making company that required a six week training class before one could become an effective rag salesperson. Now, think about selling trucks worth many tens of thousands of dollars all with complicated body arrangements and more. It seems silly to compare the two. But in some stores I have seen there wasn't much in the way of training prior to letting the salesperson go out and start talking to potential clients. A better plan is in order.

Since the mid-1990s, all of the major auto makers have really become focused on requiring training through their dealerships. To ensure that is happening they provide the training and insist that dealerships comply with it. They are not doing this for the fun of it, but instead to have better trained salespeople talking about their products. By controlling this through their dealerships, they feel they have more control of this training and trust that it benefits all parties in the process. This is good, but there needs to be more. Areas include hands-on, personal level training like touching, feeling, and experiencing for themselves, and participating with a group as well. You need a balance between the classroom and out in the field.

My Own Training Experience

Prior to the auto business I had a reasonable amount of job experience with several companies and they all required and offered training to one degree or another. What was interesting to me in entering the auto business is how little training there was and how little interest there was in providing it. I entered the auto business as a salesperson in 1972 and even then the factories had training materials and movies that could be viewed, but rarely were.

I wanted to know everything there was to know, so I watched every one of those cassette movies until I almost had them memorized. Then I asked the general manager for any other materials and listened to the ones he personally used when he got into the business. These were LP records mainly with some motivational speakers from outside the business. But there was one set from a guy who was from the auto business and I learned so much from him off those records.

I took them home, sat in a chair with a notepad, and listened over and over again taking every note I could to absorb the message. I sought out everything I could find about sales at the public library. This is where I first found two of my favorite books, *How I Raised Myself From Failure To Success In Selling* by Frank Bettger and *How To Win Friends and Influence People* by Dale Carnegie. These books and many others helped me greatly. I applied everything I could from all of those different materials. Little did I know that I was preparing myself to teach all of this in the near future.

Learning is something I have always loved and continue to love to this day. It has been my experience with many people that they are not nearly as motivated on their own to learn. The main reason is desire, I think. They don't have the drive to want to know because of how they see what they do. Many have a job and do as little as they can to get by. Others do a bit more. But it is rare in my own observation of many hundreds of employees at various firms to find those self-motivated souls who seek out learning anywhere near the degree I did myself. I needed to know, so I found the knowledge. It has made all the difference to me.

It's a good thing I studied. Within just over two years, I became the sales manager in charge of training for the sales department. Regular training meetings began once a week. As I hired a salesperson, they could not talk to a customer until they had studied for about two weeks and were able to give an effective walk around presentation to me. I figured that if they could give it to me, they could give it to anyone with even more confidence. These new hires would be sequestered in the training room watching videos, reading brochures, and then going through each vehicle with a fine tooth comb. It was a pretty effective training.

One of the biggest things I wanted to impart in the training was the fun of learning, so I tried everything I could think of to make it fun and have fun with it. That was the largest challenge with the older experienced staff, but persistence prevailed in the long run. Old dogs can learn new tricks.

This training predilection continued when I began my first commercial truck operation in 1989 and even took on a whole new level in 1995 with the creation of my Commercial Trucks 101 class. As a result of that I have given that class in commercial truck training to over a thousand salespeople all over California. After the beginning in 1989, I have developed other training and systems to help dealers deal with training in this field more effectively.

Commercial Truck Training Is Different

Yes, commercial truck training is different. It is different because a commercial truck is generally a combination of a chassis and a body from different manufacturers. You might be a *Ford* dealer and have an F250 box delete chassis and it could have a Service Body from a variety of manufacturers, made with a wide variety of materials, with an even wider variety of options, or it could have a Flatbed, Stakebed, Van Body, Contractor Body, Ferrier Body, Dump Body, and more all with the same variety of manufacturers, materials, and options. *Ford* cannot help you with training on that. They can only help you with training on the chassis. The combination of the body and the chassis is what makes this a commercial truck and there is much more to learn about the variety of bodies and applications, as well as the aspects of loading, center of gravity, and much more.

The body companies can be of assistance in some training, but it is often limited to their particular products and services. But it is going to be up to the dealer, general manager, and/or Commercial Truck Department manager to ensure that adequate training is provided to have the best staff possible and to have the best chance for success and profitability. We recommend combining the chassis manufacturer training along with all the other resources you can find. The better a staff is trained, the better the opportunity for success across the board.

The Body Companies or Manufacturers

One of the best ways to get some good training is to go to several truck body manufacturers' or distributor's sites and take a tour of their facilities. It is a great way to see how the bodies are made and to see a lot of bodies in one place in various stages of completion. Many also have training facilities and can give some classroom training as well.

In my long experience, Knapheide Manufacturing, the largest truck body manufacturer, has the best training. If you can, arrange to attend their multi-annual distributor training class which is about a week in duration. It is stellar as far as I'm concerned. I've attended training at other facilities and found good training as well, so take all you can because it will all be of benefit.

I also highly recommend touring auto manufacturer assembly facilities for those who have not had the opportunity. I've been to about five different ones and learned something at every one.

The body companies and manufacturers are usually more than willing to come to your facility and hold training classes for your staff. I recommend taking advantage of all the training that is available from all these sources.

Other Training Companies

There are many outside concerns that do training. Commercial Truck Success is one and there are others that can be of great benefit.

Some of this training will be provided at no charge and other training will come at a cost, but I recommend doing what is necessary to get the best training you can. Think of it this way. How much is one lost deal? How about one a month? Then consider even more losses than this that can come from inadequate training. An easy way is to establish a budget and let it accrue to be used as needed toward superior training.

Types of Training

Product Knowledge
The most obvious need of training would be in product knowledge. That is actually the easiest to get, the least expensive, and is of definite value and need. This includes the truck and the various body applications.

Sales Skills
Sales skills training is one of the most important training opportunities. It is not nearly as inexpensive as product training, but can be even more valuable by being able to close more sales because of increased skill and confidence.

Body Application/Commercial Truck Aspects
This training is also of high importance. We find that this training helps close more deals than any other due to depth of knowledge a person can gather about what bodies go on what chassis, how to be creative in body selection, weights and measures, and much more. There's nothing worse than selling the wrong body or wrong combination of chassis and body. It kills a lot of potential future sales, too. People

115

will have questions, they will need good answers. They will have needs and will need qualified and skilled salespeople to guide them to the best solution for those needs.

It is interesting that it is just as easy to oversell as to undersell when it comes to helping the customer choose the right truck chassis and body combination. Underselling can create overloading problems, and overselling can close your market since the higher the price, the less the market, and more important than this is the maintenance costs are also dramatically higher.

There is no such thing as the truck that will do everything. The best choice is to give the customer the best combination for what they intend to use it for and this requires knowledge and skill through training.

Prospecting and Customer Relation Management
This training will help salespeople be more successful at finding the best prospects, thus allowing for increased sales and follow up opportunities. Standing around waiting for someone to come into the dealership is not the best plan for the Commercial Truck Department.

Governmental Regulations/Driving Requirements
There is a lot to learn and know about various governmental regulations that apply to commercial trucks and commercial truck drivers. The CDL or commercial driver's license is one very important item to know about and know when it is required by whom and why. Driver's logs and other driver information can be of great value. Licensing requirements, safety inspections, and reporting

are also important to have knowledge of. In short, there is much to know about the commercial truck world as it relates to the city, county, state, and federal governments.

Inspirational and Motivational Training

We think it is equally important to include inspirational and motivational training in your training schedule. There is nothing quite like being inspired and it can enhance performance at the same time across the board.

On the Job Training

This is the training that is done on the job, to give instruction and feedback in and around actual performance. Doing is the best training possible, with success, of course.

CHAPTER SEVEN

THE
BUSINESS OFFICE

Overview

I t could go without saying, but I cannot allow that because the business office can either be a key partner, a neutral party, or a damaging critic. I have experienced all of these, and I highly recommend the key partner version. Here are some thoughts about how to help create a key partnership with the business office.

Get It Right

The office is all about organization, paying bills, billing clients, accounting, reports, filing, payroll, and more. What they want in every case is accuracy and the second thing they want is a smooth operation.

I know that a commercial truck operation is a different enough animal that it can easily cause headaches for the business office. Many times the pay plans are different, the inventory is different—especially considering the separate body with its separate invoice, and so on. Quite often the deals are different in that they may be going to lenders that are not normally used in retail. Then there are different forms that are required with commercial trucks, such as weight slips, and more.

There are many ways that the Commercial Truck Department is different enough that friction can result if the proper attention to detail is missed. The Commercial Truck Department must take charge of ensuring that the business office has every form they may need, that the deals are clean with minimal follow up issues, that all communication with the business office is clear, and that excellent paper trails are created when things are changed.

Of all the things I just listed, I would have to say it is the paper trails that can be the most important, and this has been true in my experience. One of the most blatant areas is in changes in the body, or body swaps, body removals to the ground, and so on. I've even gone so far as to make full page diagrams with arrows to make it as clear as possible to the office what changed, why, when, and how much. I've also seen where in doing this effectively, it saved the day later on when we had to look back at something and the trail was there to follow. Guessing will not do in the business office. It must be accurate and thorough.

Sometimes a unit is being purchased or traded or some other reason where monies are being transferred, checks expedited, and more. This is where the business office can be a friend or a foe. Unless, as the commercial truck manager, you have the full and obvious support of the owner where you could be seen as doing no wrong, I suggest doing everything you can to develop great relationships in the office. You will need them.

One of the ways of building those relationships is not being needy. Instead, be a giver. Buy the office lunch once in a while, give them cards on special holidays, or little gifts you found on your last trip. There are many ways to express your appreciation like this and one of the easiest and most effective is to say thank you and treat them with gratitude. Smile. Compliment them. It doesn't matter if they're male or female, everyone loves a sincere compliment. In fact, they crave it. Everyone wants to be appreciated. In fact, they crave it. Everyone wants to be respected including respecting their time and energy. In fact, they crave it.

You will find that with these suggestions, you will have such a relationship with the business office that those idiosyncrasies of the Commercial Truck Department are no longer a negative, but instead a positive. I've seen where the business manager stands up for the Commercial Truck Department if being attacked by another manager within the store. That, my friends is a massive success!

SUMMARY

What I've tried to present here is a design of an effective and profitable commercial truck operation within a retail dealership environment. In some ways, it is like a square peg in a round hole, or so it would seem. Yet in my mind it is a perfect fit as long as the uniqueness is appreciated and embraced. To segregate the department and have it feel separate is not in the best interests of the dealership as a whole. I don't think any department within a dealership is an island and all departments need each other more than they may think.

If you have been considering adding a commercial truck operation to your dealership, this book should have helped to make it clear about the potential. I've given a good deal of philosophy on how to effectively integrate and appreciate this type of operation, while pointing out the differences and how to make use of them. What I have presented has been tested and proven many times, so I am certain it will work for any dealer that chooses to follow this plan. At the same time, it is not the only way of doing it. One thing I've become clear on in my growing wisdom is that there is no one way … but there is your way, my way, and their way. They are all ways. My way is offered here and can be just as successful for you if you want it to be.

I've seen a commercial truck operation done many different ways. Many are missing some of the ingredients that also help create a healthy dealership, and instead create disharmony on several levels. This is unnecessary and counterproductive. If I were a dealer, my thought would be on building the whole as a team focused on the same objective and also enhancing and protecting the goose that lays the golden egg. The ideas and plans I've talked about are focused here and always will be. My agenda is always to enhance the dealer and their business. It is a complicated and cash crazy business enough without causing additional issues with bad choices and segregated departments.

The Advantages

There are many advantages of having an effective and profitable Commercial Truck Department.

- The first is additional revenue and profits. Not shifting it around from one place to another, but creating new revenue and new profits that did not exist before.

- If you're not now in this market, you will find it to be a unique market that is fiercely loyal. Unlike the retail market that moves like the stock market, the commercial truck market loves relationships.

They love being taken care of so they don't have to think about it. When you stop taking care of them, they will leave and never come back. It is all about relationships here.

- It is a regional market.

- Grow all parts of your dealership by adding an effective and profitable Commercial Truck Department. In turn, you will grow your Service Department rather dramatically, along with parts, body shop, detail, financing, and insurance. In some respects, this might be more important than the commercial truck sales.

- More retail sales. In my opinion, an effective and profitable Commercial Truck Department will average only 25% upfitted truck sales and the other 75% will be incremental retail sales. These numbers may vary, but in no case should the upfitted exceed 50% and be called effective. The reason for this is again, relationships. As we build a relationship with a business, it is a natural thing to encourage their employees to buy, and use our services, along with the personal vehicles of the business owners and managers.

- Marketing. Via the Commercial Truck Department, we take advantage of a business to business marketing approach and prospecting leads the way. It is active marketing, rather than passive as most advertising is. We go to them, rather than waiting for them to come to us. We do other active marketing like offsite displays, events, and trade shows.

- Internet marketing. This operation lends itself to some very effective Internet marketing using various Internet tools such as a website, blog, social media, and newsletters. As the relationships are built, this continues to grow. The *YouTube* opportunities in commercial alone are staggering because there are so few on *YouTube* with commercial trucks. There are many Internet marketing opportunities.

- Factory programs. Several manufacturers have specific financial as well as other assistance for those that focus on the commercial truck market. These programs can aid with flooring assistance, co-op advertising, demo reimbursements, marketing tools, and much more. I recommend taking full advantage of all the factory programs they have to offer.

- Better markup and profit potentials. The retail market has seen margins and profits eroding from new vehicles for a long time. The commercial truck market is unique enough to have substantially higher margins on new vehicles because of the body application. Two markups are better than one, right?

- Used commercial sales Just as in the retail dealership, the used vehicle profits are generally leading the way, and in commercial this is even more so. There are huge profits to be made in an effective Commercial Truck Department that puts good focus on finding and selling used upfits. They are harder to come by than on the retail side, but substantially more profitable as well.

- It is not always, but most often is a recession-resistant market. The people who buy commercial trucks need them to run their businesses.

- An exciting future. Hybrid commercial trucks are here. Electric and Fuel Cell commercial trucks are here, too, and there is more alternative energy and alternative designs coming in the near future. It's an exciting time to get into this market.

- Product improvements. The vehicles are improving, the bodies are improving. As we move forward, there will only be more of this, allowing us to offer better and better quality to our customers. From the time I got involved in commercial trucks to now the positive changes have been astounding.

- Competition. Or, I should say, lack of competition. It is easy to be a leader in commercial trucks. If I can do it, anyone can.

Fear and Knowledge

Some may be fearful about commercial truck inventory and other aspects of this kind of operation, but knowledge will overcome fear. What I've tried my best to give you in this book is a certain knowledge and a common sense approach to commercial inventory and managing this kind of operation.

Commercial truck inventory does require a bit more expertise than common retail inventory, but it is worth the investment in time and energy to learn about it. It requires a bit more expertise, interest in the market, and relationships with other dealers in the same market. There are major profits to be made and there is also risk of loss. Knowledge and skill will always overcome the fear.

There is also excitement in something new to learn and grow into and I think that is a healthy way to approach this market. The opportunities for dealership growth are relatively few and this commercial truck market can be a real benefit to dealership growth.

Take Charge!

It is my desire that the information provided in this book will encourage you to make a decision to get into the commercial truck market with some confidence and commitment, or to purposely avoid it. It is not for everyone.

If you see the potential that I've described here, I recommend seizing the opportunity and learning more. You may certainly give us a call and we would be happy to discuss it further with you.

Get excited about commercial because it is exciting and lucrative at the same time. Enjoy the journey.

ADDENDUM

Some resources for further knowledge, training, or consulting:

Below are some training and consulting resources beyond the chassis manufacturer and body companies that you might deal with. This is only a sampling and is not intended to be a complete list.

Commercial Truck Success. Consulting, training, and our expertise at having built highly successful commercial truck departments within retail dealerships. See more about some of those services at www.ctsdealer.net. There is a reference site with some free resources at www.comtrk.com. See our popular blog at www.ctsblog.net, and a daily inspirational message blog at www.ctsdaily.net.

Upward Trend Management Services, LLC. This is our Internet marketing business of which we serve many commercial truck dealers via our Trend Setter Package with a separate commercial truck website, blog, social media, email newsletter, video, YouTube, and consulting. See more at www.UpwardTrend.org.

Truck Marketing Institute (TMI). Great learning resource about commercial trucks, especially medium duty. See more at www.TMITraining.com.

Commercial Truck Training & Consulting by Coach Ken Taylor. Ken and his team are experts at commercial sales training and have been doing training with most of the chassis manufacturers for many years. We highly recommend Ken Taylor and his team. Call Ken at 904-535-9996, or email him at ken@coachkenttaylor.com, and see more about his training expertise and resources at www.CommercialTruckTraining.com.

Joe Verde Sales & Management Training. Joe and his worldwide team have been doing sales and management training for decades. See more at www.JoeVerde.com

Jeffrey Gitomer. Jeffrey is the world leader in sales training. Through his many books, in-depth website, audio and video, webinars, and now multiplying his own skills through his Gitomer Certified Advisor worldwide team, Jeffrey's skills and wisdom are available. We cannot recommend Jeffrey Gitomer enough. See more at www. Gitomer.com, and access his Certified Advisors at www. GitomerCertifiedAdvisors.com. Don't forget to sign up for his famous Sales Caffeine weekly email newsletter! You can register at www.Gitomer.com. Plus, he has built an online resource of webiners, videos, audio and video books, and much more at www.GitomerVT.com.

Outstand. Associated with Jeffrey Gitomer, this is a communication tool to help you stand out and apart from the crowd. See more at www.outstand.com.

The Success Training Network (TSTN). This is a great resource for full length motivational and other training by industry experts. It is well worth checking out. See more at www.tstn.com

Jim Rohn. He is listed as America's Business Philosopher. We love anything Jim Rohn. He was a master communicator. See his products and resources at www.JimRohn.com.

The John Maxwell Company. John C. Maxwell is the leading authority on leadership and management training and information. He's published more than 60 books, has a wealth of resources on his website at www.JohnMaxwell.com, and now has a worldwide network of Certified Team Members for training using John Maxwell's products called The John Maxwell Team. See more about that team and find someone in your area at www.JohnMaxwellGroup.com. We love John Maxwell's insight and common sense approach to creating better leaders and managers.

Dale Carnegie Training. One of the earliest business training organizations. Dale wrote the book on it. See more at www.DaleCarnegie.com.

Success Magazine. Now with a lot of resources. See more at www.Success.com.

Selling Power. Website and magazine. See more at www.SellingPower.com.